Foodimentary

CELEBRATING 365 FOOD HOLIDAYS
WITH CLASSIC RECIPES

JOHN-BRYAN HOPKINS

creator of Foodimentary.com

Brimming with creative inspiration, how-to projects, and useful information to enrich your everyday life, Quarto Knows is a favorite destination for those pursuing their interests and passions. Visit our site and dig deeper with our books into your area of interest: Quarto Creates, Quarto Cooks, Quarto Homes, Quarto Lives, Quarto Drives, Quarto Explores, Quarto Gifts, or Quarto Kids.

First published in 2017 by Wellfleet Press, an imprint of The Quarto Group,
142 West 36th Street, 4th Floor, New York, NY 10018, USA
T (212) 779-4972 **F** (212) 779-6058 **www.QuartoKnows.com**

Wellfleet Press titles are also available at discount for retail, wholesale, promotional, and bulk purchase. For details, contact the Special Sales Manager by email at specialsales@quarto.com or by mail at The Quarto Group, Attn: Special Sales Manager, 401 Second Avenue North, Suite 310, Minneapolis, MN 55401, USA.

For Rhonda and Sjon, and in memory of Johnny, as well as to every single fan and follower of Foodimentary, especially my early fans who helped me find my voice and sharpen my message that all food is worth celebrating.

Unless otherwise indicated below, all photos are Courtesy of the Library of Congress.
Pages 14, 128, 230, 309, 312 © Classic Stock / Alamy Stock Photo
Pages 61, 81, 99, 129, 232, 249, 318, 327 © Shutterstock
Page 248 © Prismatic Pictures / Bridgeman Images
Page 304 © Look and Learn / Bridgeman Images

10 9 8 7 6 5 4 3 2 1

ISBN: 978-1-57715-153-1

Cover Design: Merideth Harte
Interior Design: Jen Cogliantry

Printed in China

Contents

It's Foodimentary, My Dear!

Hello, my name is John-Bryan Hopkins, and I'm here to tell you that just one word can change your life . . . for me, that word is Foodimentary. My story begins in 2005, while cooking with friends and talking about how I wanted to do something different with my life. Food blogging was getting big, and I knew I could do it but just needed a spark of inspiration to get me started on my journey. After dinner, my guests and I started to play a game about what to name my imaginary blog. Drinks were had, and, well, suffice it to say, the game became a bit silly. Suddenly, I blurted out, "Listen, I don't want to do a blog about myself and what I'm cooking, but, instead,

something about discovering and celebrating food. I want a blog dedicated to the elements of food that people have long forgotten . . . it's foodimentary, my dear!" Instantaneously, a friend agreed, "I love that word!"

We immediately ran to my laptop and searched for other blogs that might have that name. Luckily, and to my amazement, there were no results. Zero! My heart stopped. The limitless possibilities quickly began to present themselves. I had just created a potential blog name, and I envisioned myself relating to the world what my blog was about. I began to be inspired—I now needed to figure out exactly what it should be. I bought the Foodimentary.com domain address and spent the next couple of months pondering what to write. I felt that food blogging tended to be more about the person writing the blog, which was not my style, than about interesting food facts. This newly invented word was my baby, and I needed to think about my blog's concept thoroughly. I wanted to do something different. Foodimentary, I thought, needed to be the antiblog, in a way. I wanted to inform readers, every day, about food and its history with the goal of altering their perception of food . . . or at least that is what I hoped. I wanted—and still want today—Foodimentary to be about those "aha" food moments.

I spent several months getting inspired, reading and researching food facts and gathering food-related knowledge. I filled four spiral notebooks, in addition to a laptop, to the brim with facts. I began to curate Foodimentary moments in my blog using those nuggets of information every day. My plan and vision were beginning to take shape. I designed my first blog using an understated aesthetic on Blogger. My first posts were a mix of fun food facts and vintage photos of dishes and ingredients that interested me. Within five weeks my blog became popular, but to be truthful—and I hate to sound like I am bragging—it really became *super* popular and was soon receiving thousands upon thousands of hits a day.

Most people would, understandably, be proud and strut about like cockerel; however, that is not who I am. Truth be told, I was a bit scared, since I felt that I was just doing my job, which was to define what Foodimentary meant, and it was working. My blog became the front man, and I was the hidden wizard in the background. I never thought I would have to come out from behind the curtain—but that is exactly what soon happened!

Always wanting to enhance and build my Foodimentary brand, I scrutinized every blog I could find to determine what people liked about food and food history. Not only did it help my blogging, but it also allowed me to devise an overall blueprint for what Foodimentary should cover. I decided that when it comes to food facts, people want simple sentences about the celebratory food. I also decided that there was *absolutely* no room for negative responses and that I did not want a blog with screaming opinions. No, I thought, it is better to have four or five simple facts about food every day along with a searchable database on the blog.

While I was building and shaping my blog, a little thing called "social media" started to develop. There was Loopt, Gowalla, BrightKite, Foursquare, Facebook (of course), and a blossoming new platform called Twitter. Since it took only about thirty minutes to write my

Foodimentary blog entries, I thought a social-media platform for Foodimentary would be a perfect marriage. So off I went, joining every social-media outlet I could and posting on them daily. Unfortunately, Facebook soon became a disaster. I developed a huge following and a great audience, but someone thought I was a "bot" (a fake account), and in one simple click my more than forty-five thousand followers were quickly erased. Needless to say, my heart was broken; therefore, I currently do not use Facebook that much—yes, this is the downer moment in my story.

I joined Twitter using a random name in 2007, just to see how it worked. Although it functioned like many other social-media platforms, I was a bit hesitant to pursue it further for fear that it might have been a fleeting trend. Finally, in 2008, I joined as Foodimentary. I tweet you not: within just four weeks, I was among the top 1000 Twitter accounts in the world. Within four months, I was in the top 100 accounts. Needless to say, I had found my platform! I knew from my research that one of the most popular and trending topics in the food category was food holidays—which, to be honest, really is the proverbial gift that keeps on giving—since there is some type of holiday celebrating food for every day of the year! I immediately thought that incorporating food holidays into

Foodimentary would be a perfect complement, so I went to work compiling a list of days and their corresponding food holidays.

At the time, there really was not much on the Web about food holidays, so I scoured newspaper and periodical archives for weeks. National holidays can be created by anyone, and, in fact, many companies and corporations create them to market and sell their brands. Unfortunately, in our modern consumer society, many of us have become a bit jaded over these faux holidays. We see through the gimmick, but social media absolutely loves these holidays and cannot get enough of them! Today, we can find celebrations that run the gamut from esoteric National Turkey Neck Soup Day (March 30) to mainstream National Chocolate Chip Cookie Day (August 4). It was important to establish what a "national" food holiday was for Foodimentary. I define it as a type of collective food nostalgia, or food memory, which maybe includes dishes, smells, ingredients, and textures from our childhoods; home-cooked meals by relatives; or perhaps forgotten food fads from our past. Having said this, there were some food holidays I just did not like. I remember coming across National Frozen Food Day (March 6) and thinking, "Who wants to celebrate frozen food in March?" so I switched it to National Oreo Cookie Day. I found about two hundred food holidays worth celebrating, but some, like National Lard Day, were definitely not going to happen on my watch, so I started finding foods that *I* wanted to celebrate. My mantra became: Celebrate Food Every Day, and I took it upon myself to come up with the remaining 366 food holidays—we cannot forget leap year!

While I continued to blog and test new areas for Foodimentary, I started gaining attention within social media. I remember reading an online article about a popular and influential Twitter award: the Shorty Awards, which is the equivalent of an Oscar within the Twitter community. To my surprise, I won in the food category in 2009! It felt like I was a part of something that had the potential to be big. Fast forward to the next year, and I was the first Twitter account to win twice! My food holiday calendar was then adopted by Google a couple of years later, leaving me in awe and speechless. Foodimentary has been featured in *Time* magazine as one of the top 140 Twitter accounts, on Mashable.com as one of the top 55 Twitter accounts, as well as in the *Wall Street Journal*, the *New York Times*, Epicurious.com, the Food Network, and many others. The writers are curious to know more about me, how Foodimentary was started, and how I helped to create and promote the celebration of food holidays. Although the accolades are inspiring

and extremely rewarding, personally I feel my job has been accomplished if I just get one retweet or if my website is shared.

This brings me to the present. My days now are filled with organizing my food holiday calendar three to four months in advance. Usually, people who are creating a new holiday will put the word out, and I will then check to see if there is a conflict on any particular days. I keep a record of every day to see if it was popular over the past years, and if it wasn't, then the day is open for a new holiday. I continue to build and develop the best food holiday calendar possible. I seldom retire a food holiday; instead, I lower the holiday by removing "National." Other issues I come across are duplicate days. For example, Canada, Great Britain, and many other countries have their own food holidays, but in the social media world, they like to have one day for each food. I was told December 21 was wrong for National Hamburger Day, so I searched around on the Web and found that Iran had its own date for celebrating hamburgers. If people celebrate a food en masse and enjoy that "day," then let them celebrate it, I say! After all, yesterday's Low Carb Day may give way to Greek Yogurt Day, and so on—Viva Taco Tuesday!

I finally decided it was time to write a book that included the current food celebrations along with classic recipes. From my early days of blogging, people have been asking for a book of food holidays. Over time, reflection has taught me what a Foodimentary book should be, and I hope you enjoy the following pages as much as I have enjoyed gathering the interesting facts and histories of some of our most famous dishes. Arguably, a food book is not complete without recipes, so my wish is that readers will be able to learn something new about a favorite food or dish and then cook it. I placed my own twist on the many recipes in the following pages, and my hope is that readers will turn to the page that contains their birthday or anniversary and perhaps make that recipe, and the day, a little bit more special.

If someone were to have told me that I would be blogging for over a decade, participating in the early days of social media, serving as an influential voice within the food community, and becoming the godfather of food holidays, I never would have believed it. I've always considered my work to be one simple task: to use my word "Foodimentary" as a means of spreading my love of food throughout the world. I love my job, and I hope this book conveys that. The best thing I've learned to do along this journey—and what I encourage others to do—is to be honest and true to one's idea or brand. Foodimentary is the front man, and I am just the guy who is holding it in his hands, waiting for it to turn into a butterfly and fly away.

SPRING

MARCH

RANCH

Food Celebrations This Month

National Fresh Celery Month

National Noodle Month

National Flour Month

National Frozen Food Month

National Nutrition Month

National Peanut Month

National Sauce Month

National Caffeine Awareness Month

March 1

PEANUT BUTTER LOVER'S DAY

{ *Three sisters eating peanut butter and jelly sandwiches for lunch, ca. 1950s.*

The earliest version of peanut butter dates all the way back to the Aztecs and Incas, who crushed peanuts into a paste. Although the United States is the world's biggest consumer of peanut butter, it was a Canadian, Marcellus Edson, who first patented the creamy spread in 1884. Early health food pioneer Dr. John Harvey Kellogg used to serve peanut butter to his patients in his Michigan sanitarium. Later, it officially debuted at the St. Louis World's Fair in 1904.

PEANUT BUTTER

March 2
BANANA CREAM PIE DAY

{ *Early banana importers and distributers were mostly Italian immigrants, ca. 1900.*

Not until after the Civil War were bananas commonplace for most Americans. Until then, only the major cities sold the "exotic" and easily perishable fruit. Once transportation became faster, it didn't take long before bananas were available to everyone almost year round. Many early recipes from the 1890s give different variations of a cake layered with cream and sliced bananas. By 1929, the Nabisco company began producing Vanilla Wafers (the precursor to Nilla Wafers) and featured a banana pudding recipe on the box that used the cookies as a piecrust base. Needless to say, bananas and Nilla Wafers have since become inseparable.

March 3
COLD CUTS DAY

Cold cuts are sliced, precooked, or cured meat, often in the form of sausages or meat loaves. Usually, they are served on sandwiches or as part of a platter with cheese and crackers. They are most commonly sold vacuum-packed at the grocery store or sliced to order at the deli. Most presliced cold cuts are higher in fat, nitrates, and sodium than those that are sliced to order.

March 4
POUND CAKE DAY

Pound cakes have been delighting us since the early 1700s. A British creation, the original recipe called for a pound each of flour, sugar, butter, and eggs, hence its name. By the middle of the 1800s, the recipe began to change, as cooks added various flavorings such as vanilla, cocoa powder, lemon juice, and—a Southern specialty—cream cheese.

Pound Cake

Makes 24 servings

INGREDIENTS

Nonstick cooking spray
1 pound (4 sticks) butter
1 pound (2½ cups) sugar
10 eggs, separated
1 pound (3⅓ cups) all-purpose flour
2 tablespoons brandy

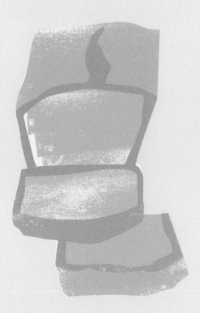

DIRECTIONS

1. Preheat the oven to 350°F. Spray a Bundt pan or 9 x 5-inch loaf pan with cooking spray and set aside.

2. In the bowl of a standing mixer or using a handheld mixer, cream butter and sugar on medium-high speed until light and fluffy, 3 to 5 minutes.

3. Add the egg yolks one at a time, beating between each addition, until thick and lemon colored.

4. In a large bowl, beat the egg whites on high speed until stiff peaks form.

5. Add the flour, egg whites, and brandy to the butter mixture, beating vigorously for 5 minutes.

6. Bake for 75 minutes, or until a skewer inserted into the center of the cake comes out clean.

March 5
CHEEZ DOODLE DAY

Accounts vary, but it's thought that cheese puffs began to be produced in the 1930s. One of the most popular brands, Cheez Doodles by Wise Foods, started in the early 1950s. Cheez Doodles are said to be one of the only packaged snack foods that Julia Child would eat.

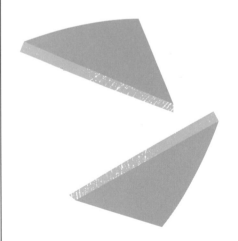

March 6
OREO COOKIE DAY

In 1912, Nabisco debuted its newest cookie creation, the "Oreo Biscuit," which was first sold to a grocer in Hoboken, New Jersey. The name and design may have changed over the years, but the cookie is still delicious and continues to be a smash hit more than one hundred years later!

FUN FOOD FACTS

The origin of the name Oreo is still a mystery today.

Oreos are the world's best-selling cookie.

There was a lemon meringue flavor when Oreos first came to the market, but it was discontinued due to weak sales.

March 7
CEREAL DAY

In 1863, James Caleb Jackson invented America's first cold breakfast cereal, Granula, which consisted of graham flour pieces that needed to be soaked overnight in milk. (Later, Dr. John Harvey Kellogg created a variation and called it Granola to be different from Jackson's.) Prior to this invention, most Americans ate a portion of meat and eggs for breakfast or porridge, which the early colonists brought with them from England. By 1900, Kellogg came out with Corn Flakes, and by 1910 the Quaker Oats Company began to produce Puffed Rice and Puffed Wheat. In 1920, Wheaties debuted, with its famous slogan "Breakfast of Champions." In 1940, General Mills introduced CheeriOats, which was quickly renamed Cheerios, and in 1979 Honey Nut Cheerios, the brand's most popular version, was introduced. By the 1970s, many fruit-flavored and sugary cereals were available to consumers. No matter what your favorite, here's to morning cereals!

March 8
PEANUT CLUSTER DAY

A peanut cluster is a type of candy that mixes melted chocolate and peanuts. These crunchy treats are a perfect combination of sweet and salty deliciousness. There are several versions of peanut clusters, including caramel clusters, butterscotch clusters, and chocolate peanut clusters.

FUN FOOD FACT

Peanuts have more antioxidants than grapes, green tea, tomatoes, spinach, and carrots.

March 9
CRAB DAY

Although historical evidence shows that crabs were known to and eaten by ancient Greeks and Romans, it appears they weren't big fans of the tasty crustaceans. The early American colonists used crabs in stews and soups; however, by the nineteenth century, crab recipes could be found everywhere. Many people associate crabs with the state of Maryland and the Chesapeake Bay area, where blue crabs live abundantly and have long served as a food staple for the region.

March 10
RANCH DRESSING DAY

Whether it's used as a savory salad dressing or a dip for vegetables, chicken wings, onion rings, and more, ranch dressing is an American favorite. Steve Henson, originally a contract plumber in Alaska, first developed the recipe, along with his wife, when they moved to their Hidden Valley Ranch in California in the early 1950s. An instant success, Henson sold guests both bottled dressing and seasoning packets to make the dressing at home. Soon the dressing was available nationwide.

March 11
"EAT YOUR NOODLES" DAY

Who created noodles? It's a million-dollar question still being debated today, with many different cultures claiming credit. Many food historians believe that the Chinese were first to invent them, as the earliest written record of noodles dates from the East Han dynasty between A.D. 25 to 220. Nowadays, noodles and noodle variations can be found in the cuisines of countless cultures. Today, we celebrate the noodle in all its glory—whether it's a simple spaghetti aglio e olio or a warming bowl of ramen noodles.

March 12
MILKY WAY DAY

First created in 1923 by Frank C. Mars (founder of Mars, Incorporated) in Minneapolis, Minnesota, Milky Way chocolate bars were based on the popular chocolate-malted milkshake. Originally, there was a chocolate version and a vanilla version, which for a couple of years were sold packaged together. The vanilla Milky Way was renamed Forever Yours and produced until 1979. It was reintroduced as Milky Way Dark in 1989, and the name changed again in 2000 to Milky Way Midnight.

FUN FOOD FACT
Unlike the American version, the smaller, lighter European Milky War bar has no caramel filling and can actually float in milk.

March 13
CHICKEN SOUP DAY

One of America's well-known culinary traditions is no doubt Campbell's Chicken Noodle Soup, which debuted in 1934 as Noodle with Chicken Soup. After a popular on-air personality incorrectly said the name as "Chicken Noodle Soup," customers began clamoring for the new soup, and soon the famous soup was rebranded. Opposite is an easy homemade version, but feel free to celebrate chicken and noodles in any way you like today!

Mom's Homemade Chicken Soup

Makes 6 servings

INGREDIENTS

1 tablespoon olive oil
½ cup diced carrot
½ cup diced onion
½ cup diced celery
Pinch salt
¼ teaspoon fresh thyme leaves
1 tablespoon fennel seeds
2 bay leaves
2 quarts chicken broth
4 ounces uncooked egg noodles
2 cooked boneless chicken breast
   halves, cubed
Pinch cayenne pepper
Pinch coarse-ground black pepper

DIRECTIONS

1. In a large pot or Dutch oven, heat the olive oil over medium heat. Add the carrot, onion, and celery; cook, stirring occasionally for 3 to 5 minutes, or until the onions are translucent. Stir in the salt, thyme, fennel seeds, and bay leaves.

2. Add the chicken broth, increase the heat to high, and bring the mixture to a boil. Stir in the egg noodles and cook for 3 to 5 minutes, or according to package directions. Stir in the cubed chicken, reduce heat to medium-low, and simmer for 3 minutes, or until chicken is warmed through.

3. Season with cayenne and black pepper. Remove bay leaves and serve.

March 14
POTATO CHIP DAY

Some accounts claim that the first mention of potato chips is in William Kitchiner's 1817 cookbook *The Cook's Oracle* under the name "Potatoes Fried in Slices or Shavings." There are also recipes dating from 1824 in Mary Randolf's *Virginia House-Wife*, which references Kitchiner. Popular legend also has it that in 1853 at the Moon Lake Lodge's restaurant in Saratoga Springs, New York, a disgruntled diner sent his French-fried potatoes back to the chef two times due to their large size. Frustrated, chef George Crum sliced the potatoes extra thin and heavily salted them out of frustration. Contrary to expectations, the chips were a smashing success, and soon became a regular menu item. They were packaged and sold as Saratoga Chips. Today, all kinds of flavorings, styles, and brands are available around the world.

Homemade Potato Chips

Makes 4 servings

INGREDIENTS

2 medium russet potatoes
Nonstick cooking spray
Coarse salt
Ground black pepper
Truffle oil, for garnish (optional)

DIRECTIONS

1. Preheat the oven to 425°F. Line a cookie sheet with parchment paper.

2. Slice the potatoes into ⅛-inch-thick slices. This is best done with a mandoline to ensure even slices.

3. Arrange the slices in a single layer on the prepared cookie sheet. Spray with nonstick cooking spray; sprinkle with salt and pepper. Bake for 20 minutes or until golden brown and crisp.

4. Remove the cookie sheet from the oven and garnish the chips with truffle oil, if using. Repeat the process with the remaining sliced potatoes. Serve the chips immediately, or cool and store in an airtight container.

March 15
PEANUT LOVERS' DAY

Everybody loves peanuts—so much so there's a saying: "Willpower is the ability to eat one peanut!" Peanuts account for two-thirds of all snack nuts consumed in the United States. Since they grow underground, however, they are technically considered legumes and not nuts.

FUN FOOD FACTS

Archibutyrophobia is the fear of getting peanut butter stuck to the roof of your mouth.

The peanut nickname "goober" comes from the West African Kikongo word nguba, *meaning "peanut."*

West Coasters tend to prefer crunchy peanut butter while East Coasters tend to prefer smooth.

March 16
ARTICHOKE HEART DAY

While many food historians credit the Moors in northern Africa for cultivating artichokes, the ancient Romans and Greeks grew artichokes for centuries, making them one of the oldest harvested foods. A tastier and better variant of its relative, the cardoon, artichokes are a huge Mediterranean favorite, with countless recipes to enjoy.

March 17
"EAT LIKE AN IRISHMAN" DAY

Potatoes, stews, seafood, breads . . . the list of delicious Irish foods is endless. Today, we celebrate everything Irish. *Sláinte mhaith!*

FUN FOOD FACTS

Leprechauns, famous to Ireland, are said to grant wishes to those who can catch them.

The first fish and chips was served in Dublin in the 1880s by Italian immigrants.

Saint Patrick's Day has been celebrated in North America since the late eighteenth century.

March 18
SLOPPY JOES DAY

Who invented the Sloppy Joe? Well, you guessed it: it depends on whom you ask. Some say a cook named Joe from Sioux City, Iowa, invented the dish in 1930 by adding tomato sauce to a "loose meat" sandwich—which continues to be a popular sandwich in many parts of the Midwest—while others credit Sloppy Joe's Bar in Havana, Cuba, which also served a loose-meat sandwich and whose owner, José Abeal y Otero, was nicknamed "Sloppy Joe" by English-speaking patrons, yet others claim it was at the legendary Sloppy Joe's Bar restaurant in Key West, Florida. At the end of day, let's give a huge thanks to Joe, or *muchas gracias* to José, for this delicious sandwich.

Diner-Style Sloppy Joes

Makes 4 sloppy joes

INGREDIENTS

1 tablespoon olive oil
1 green bell pepper, diced
1 cup diced red onion
½ cup diced celery
2 cloves garlic, minced
1¼ pounds ground beef
½ teaspoon salt
½ cup ketchup
3 tablespoons tomato paste
1 tablespoon soy sauce
1 tablespoon white wine vinegar
1½ tablespoons packed brown sugar
½ teaspoon thyme
Pinch cayenne pepper
Pinch ground black pepper
4 hamburger buns
¾ cup shredded Cheddar cheese

DIRECTIONS

1. Heat olive oil in a large sauté pan over medium heat. Add bell pepper, onion, celery, and garlic. Cook, stirring occasionally, until onions are translucent, about 5 minutes.

2. Add the ground beef and salt. Cook, using a wooden spoon to break up any chunks, until brown, about 5 minutes. Strain off most of the fat.

3. Add the ketchup, tomato paste, soy sauce, vinegar, brown sugar, thyme, cayenne pepper, and black pepper to the pan. Stir well to combine.

4. Lower the heat to low, cover, and simmer for 10 minutes. Adjust seasoning as necessary.

5. Serve on hamburger buns and top with cheese.

March 19
OATMEAL COOKIE DAY

With roots as Scottish and British oatcakes, the oatmeal cookie began to make an appearance around 1896 in Fannie Merritt Farmer's famous *The Boston Cooking-School Cook Book*. Billing them as a healthy cookie, the Quaker Oat Company soon advertised recipes for oatmeal cookies on the label on the back of their packaging. Our modern takeaway? Rationalize your sugar craving with this historically "healthy" cookie!

FUN FOOD FACT
The ancient Romans supposedly had to put up a very good fight against the Highland Scots when they conquered Great Britain, for the hardy warriors carried oatmeal pouches to sustain them in battle.

March 20
RAVIOLI DAY

The word "ravioli" is from the Italian word *riavvolgere*, meaning "to wrap." *Ravioli nudi*, or "naked ravioli," refers to only the filling, without the pasta. The Italian tradition is to serve vegetarian ravioli on Fridays, while meat-filled ravioli is served as either a side dish or later in the meal on other days.

FUN FOOD FACTS
Chef Boyardee started making canned ravioli in the 1930s.

"Fresh-packed" ravioli can last for several weeks, while fresh-made lasts for just a few days.

March 21
CRUNCHY TACO DAY

Although to many Americans in the 1960s and 1970s tacos were synonymous with the fast-food chain Taco Bell (created by Glen William Bell Jr. in 1964), Mexicans have been eating tacos for centuries, well before the Spaniards arrived in the sixteenth century. The origins of the word "taco" are a bit murky, but by the end of the nineteenth century, Mexican vendors were selling tacos from street stands to tourists and workers in southwestern cities and California. Today, Mexican food is as popular as ever, with an emphasis on traditional, regional, and diverse dishes.

March 22
WATER DAY

There is more fresh water stored under the ground in aquifers than on the earth's surface. Over 70 percent of an adult's body is made up of water. Of all the water on the earth, humans use about three-tenths of a percent for drinking. The recommended daily intake of water is eight cups per day, including water consumed through food. However, drinking too much water too quickly can lead to water intoxication, which is caused by a reduction in sodium levels in the blood stream—some confuse this with a "runner's high."

FUN FOOD FACT
In ideal conditions and with minimal physical exertion, humans can survive only three to five days without water. Extreme heat and physical overexertion shorten that survival period to several hours.

March 23
CHIPS AND DIPS DAY

A party or get-together is just not complete without some kind of chips and dip, the perfect combination. One of the first dips to hit the market in the early 1950s was the Lipton company's Lipton California Dip, which would later be renamed French Onion Dip in the 1960s. Today, there are all kinds of different dips, from hummus, white bean, and avocado to cheese, spinach, and buffalo chicken.

March 24
TORTILLA CHIP DAY

Many credit Rebecca Webb Carranza of Los Angeles, California, with the invention of the tortilla chip in the 1940s. She decided to cut the rejected tortillas from her mechanical tortilla machine into triangles, refry them, and then sell the chips as a snack food. However, tortilla chips have been available in many restaurants throughout Southern California since the early 1900s, as they were a perfect way of using up and selling extra tortilla dough. They did not receive much nationwide attention until the 1970s, when they branched out and became available throughout the United States.

INTERNATIONAL WAFFLE DAY

Whether enjoyed with sweet toppings, such as maple syrup and powdered sugar, or savory toppings, such as chicken or kidney stew, waffles are beloved by many different cultures. Their roots begin during the Middle Ages, when *obloyeurs* or waffle makers, would sell cooked, flat wafers called *oublies* from street carts outside churches during religious celebrations. The bread was not leavened, and the early ingredients were simply water and flour. By the fifteenth century, the first waffle irons began to be manufactured, giving way to the classic, rectangular shape. Because the new shape resembled a honeycomb—*wafla* in old French—the food became known as *wafel* in Dutch and then waffle in English. Soon sugar, milk, and eggs began to be incorporated into the mixture. The Belgian waffle, which uses yeast as a leavener, was introduced to Americans in 1964 at the New York World's Fair.

March 26
NOUGAT DAY

Modern nougat is a mixture of sucrose and corn syrup, with a whipping agent to create a fluffy texture. It was used in candy bars because it resembled the texture and flavor of ice cream, which is why early candy bars were commonly served frozen to seem more like ice cream. The candy bar 3 Musketeers, among the most popular nougat candy bars of the twentieth century, first consisted of three flavors: chocolate, vanilla, and strawberry.

March 27
WORLD WHISKEY DAY

Whisky and *whiskey* are the same liquor. In the United States and Ireland, the word is spelled "whiskey," while in Britain and other countries, it is spelled "whisky." There are more than five thousand types of single malt whiskey. The dark color of this distilled alcoholic beverage comes from the compounds in the wooden barrels in which it is aged, and the barrels made from American white oak are claimed to produce the tastiest variety.

March 28
BLACK FOREST CAKE DAY

From the Black Forest region in southern Germany—which is known for its sour cherries and the cherry-flavored brandy Kirsch or Kirschwasser—comes this beloved cake. Black Forest Cake originated in the sixteenth century, when chocolate first started to be added to desserts, and has been an international hit ever since. Josef Keller is considered the creator of our modern version when, in 1915, he baked a cake that he called *Schwarzwderkirschtorte*, or Black Forest Cherry Torte. He later gave his recipe book to his assistant, August Schaefer, whose son has kept the original recipe alive ever since.

March 29
CHIFFON CAKE DAY

Chiffon cakes are known for their light and fluffy texture, which comes from using vegetable oil and egg whites instead of butter. Harry Baker, from Los Angeles, California, invented the cake in 1927, but held onto his secret recipe and sold his creation only to film stars and the legendary Brown Derby Restaurant. He eventually sold the recipe to General Mills, which published it through Betty Crocker in the late 1940s, and it immediately became a smashing success.

March 30
TURKEY NECK SOUP DAY

The neck may not seem like the most nutritious part of a turkey, but if you save and freeze them after major feasts or regular meals, they can be a very cost-effective ingredient in soups and stews later on. Although the meat is fairly tough and requires a longer cooking time than other meats, they add lots of flavor to broths with vegetables and noodles or rice.

FUN FOOD FACTS
A turkey will change the color of its head and throat depending on its mood.

A turkey's gobble can be heard a mile away.

Benjamin Franklin wanted the national bird to be a turkey and not a bald eagle.

March 31
CLAM DAY

On the opposite page is a fantastic retro recipe that celebrates one of our favorite mollusks. The popular radio and television show Kraft Music Hall made this recipe famous after broadcasting it during one of its shows in the early 1950s, when dips became all the rage. It continued to be popular well into the 1960s, but was replaced in the 1970s by salsa as America's favorite chip dip.

Classic Clam Dip

Makes 12 servings

INGREDIENTS

2 (8-ounce) packages cream cheese, at room temperature

2 (6.5-ounces) cans minced clams, drained well

¼ cup chopped shallots

½ cup chopped flat-leaf parsley

3 tablespoons lemon juice

¼ cup grated Parmesan cheese

Baguette slices, for serving

DIRECTIONS

1. Preheat the oven to 350°F. Butter a 3¾-quart oven-safe dish.

2. Mix all ingredients except the Parmesan cheese in a large bowl until well combined.

3. Spoon the dip into the prepared dish. Top with grated Parmesan.

4. Transfer to the preheated oven and bake for 25 minutes, or until the top is a light golden brown.

5. Remove and serve warm with baguette slices.

APRIL

Food Celebrations This Month

National Florida Tomato Month

National BLT Sandwich Month

National Soft Pretzel Month

National Soy Foods Month

National Grilled Cheese Month

National Garlic Month

National Egg Salad Week

April 1

NATIONAL BLT MONTH

Although the main ingredients of a bacon, lettuce, and tomato sandwich haven't changed over the years, its name has evolved. Most likely a restaurant's kitchen abbreviation for the order, the BLT was first mentioned as a club sandwich in the 1903 *Good Housekeeping Everyday Cook Book*; however, that recipe included mayonnaise and turkey. Here's a fancy updated version opposite.

FUN FOOD FACT

One of the earliest recipes for the BLT appears in Elizabeth Hiller's Calendar of Sandwiches & Beverages *(1920), which included the "Bacon and Tomato Sandwich" under September 30.*

Bruschetta alla BLT

Makes 36 bruschette

INGREDIENTS

3 ounces feta cheese

½ cup mayonnaise

1 loaf French bread,
   cut into ¾-inch-thick slices

¼ cup plus 1 tablespoon olive oil

4 tomatoes, diced

½ cup chopped fresh basil leaves

8 slices bacon, cooked and crumbled

1 clove garlic, cut in half lengthwise

Kosher salt and freshly ground pepper

DIRECTIONS

1. Preheat the oven to 300°F. In a small bowl, stir together the feta and mayonnaise until well mixed. Cover and set aside.

2. Arrange the bread slices on a parchment paper–lined baking sheet and brush with ¼ cup oil. Transfer to the oven and bake for 12 minutes or until golden and crispy.

3. In a medium mixing bowl, toss the tomatoes, basil, and bacon with the remaining 1 tablespoon oil. Set aside.

4. Rub each piece of toasted bread with the raw garlic clove. Spread with the mayo mixture and then add a spoonful of the BLT mix. Add a touch of salt and pepper to taste.

April 2
PEANUT BUTTER AND JELLY DAY

A mainstay of countless children's—and adults'—lunches, peanut butter and jelly sandwiches were referenced for the first time in the 1901 cookbook *Boston Cooking-School Magazine of Culinary Science and Domestic Economics*. During the Great Depression, peanut butter sandwiches quickly gained popularity as a cheap meal that contained protein. However, they became extremely popular after World War II, when soldiers who received peanut butter and jelly as rations returned home and brought their wartime meal with them, leading to a huge increase in peanut butter and jelly sales.

April 3
CHOCOLATE MOUSSE DAY

The French word *mousse* means "froth" or "foam," and savory mousse dishes were common in eighteenth-century France. Dessert mousses—mostly made with fruit ingredients—didn't appear until much later, in the second half of the nineteenth century. One of the first written records of chocolate mousse in the United States comes from an 1892 food exposition at Madison Square Garden in New York City, but it wouldn't be until the 1930s when chocolate mousse would become a common household dessert—around the same time chocolate pudding mixes were introduced to the market.

April 4
CHICKEN CORDON BLEU DAY

Contrary to popular belief, chicken cordon bleu is neither a very old dish nor is it from the prestigious Le Cordon Bleu cooking school. In fact, the first instance of this delicious creation dates to a 1967 recipe from the cooking section of the *New York Times*. Similar recipes using veal instead of chicken can be found a little earlier. Most likely, chicken cordon bleu was inspired by chicken Kiev, which itself was a reinvention of a French dish from the 1840s that used veal instead of chicken.

FUN FOOD FACT
The term cordon bleu *literally means "blue ribbon" in French—a reference to the sash worn by the prestigious Order of the Knights of the Holy Spirit, founded in 1578 by King Henry III of France.*

April 5
CARAMEL DAY

Hershey's introduced caramel to the American market in the 1880s, but caramel has its roots in France and Britain (called toffee), where it's been made since the early 1800s. Americans began to add milk or cream to the mix, and a new "American" version was created. The basic ingredients for an American-style caramel are sugar, milk, and butter, which are cooked at a lower temperature than their European counterparts. Butterscotch is cooked like a caramel, but uses brown sugar and butter to give it a unique taste.

April 6
CARAMEL POPCORN DAY

Caramel corn came about in the 1870s when Frederick and Louis Rueckheim, two brothers who opened a popcorn store in Chicago, started to experiment with different types of popcorn flavorings and coatings. They found that their peanut and molasses combination was a huge hit, and Cracker Jack was born.

FUN FOOD FACT
The product name Cracker Jack originated in 1896 after a sampler exclaimed, "That's a crackerjack!," which at the time was a colloquialism that meant a great product.

April 7
COFFEE CAKE DAY

Cakes, in their various forms, have been around since biblical times, with the simplest varieties made from honey, dates, or other fruits. Coffee cake evolved from a variety of cakes. The Danish came up with the earliest versions around the seventeenth century, when it became customary to enjoy a sweet bread while drinking coffee. The hole inside coffee cakes is a relatively recent innovation from the 1950s, when the Bundt pan was invented. It allowed a heavy batter to be cooked all the way through without the center remaining raw.

FUN FOOD FACT

The British version of coffee cake is a coffee-flavored sponge cake with coffee-flavored butter icing, often topped with walnuts.

Cream Cheesy Coffee Cake

Makes 2 (9-inch) cakes

INGREDIENTS

Cake

¼ cup (½ stick) butter, at room temperature

8 ounces cream cheese, at room temperature

1½ cups granulated sugar

2 eggs

½ cup milk

1 teaspoon vanilla

2 cups all-purpose flour

2 teaspoons baking powder

1 teaspoon baking soda

1 teaspoon cinnamon

¼ teaspoon ground nutmeg

½ teaspoon kosher salt

Streusel Topping

¼ cup butter

¼ cup all-purpose flour

1 cup packed brown sugar

½ teaspoon cinnamon

¼ teaspoon kosher salt

DIRECTIONS

1. Preheat the oven to 350°F. Grease and flour two 9-inch cake pans; set aside.

2. To make the cake: In a large mixing bowl with a handheld mixer, cream together the butter, cream cheese, granulated sugar, and eggs on medium speed until light and fluffy, about 3 minutes.

3. With the mixer running, add the milk and vanilla and mix an additional 2 minutes to incorporate.

4. In another large bowl, sift together the flour, baking powder, baking soda, cinnamon, nutmeg, and salt. Slowly add the dry ingredients to the wet ingredients, and mix on medium speed until incorporated, about 2 minutes total.

5. Divide mixture evenly between the prepared cake pans. Set aside while you make the topping.

6. To make the topping: In a medium bowl, mix together all the streusel ingredients and spread evenly over the top of the cake batter.

7. Transfer to the oven and bake for 20 to 25 minutes, or until golden and a toothpick inserted in the center of the cakes comes out with a few dry crumbs. Serve warm.

April 8
EMPANADA DAY

Spanning thousands of miles and many different countries, from Argentina to the Philippines, empanadas are a favorite pocket turnover dish for many people. They are believed to have originated in the sixteenth century in the northwestern province of Galicia in Spain, and it's thought that Spanish explorers then introduced empanadas to the lands they encountered. *Pan* means "bread" and *empanar* means "to coat with bread" in Spanish. Each culture has a different variation, with some empanadas using sweet fillings like raisins and fruit or savory ingredients such as meat and potatoes.

FUN FOOD FACT
Northern Indian empanadas are known as gujias. *Often distributed during* Holi, *the spring Hindu "festival of colors," they are filled with grated dried fruits, ricotta-like* khoya, *and coconut.*

April 9
CHINESE ALMOND COOKIE DAY

Typical to southern and southeastern China, these almond cookies are usually enjoyed around Chinese New Year and are given as gifts to family and friends. In some Chinese restaurants, they are served between courses to cleanse diners' palates rather than as a dessert.

April 10
CINNAMON ROLL DAY

Known as *Schnecken* in Germany, *kanelbulle* in Sweden, and Chelsea buns in England, cinnamon rolls are a bit different from their American friends. Many believe that the first cinnamon rolls were created by the Swedes, who, along with German-speaking settlers—known as the Pennsylvania Dutch—brought them to the Philadelphia region in the seventeenth century. They continue to be a Swedish national treasure and are a popular treat for *fika*, a coffee-and-dessert break during the day.

FUN FOOD FACT

Bostoninkakku ("Boston cake") is a Finnish creation, consisting of several cinnamon rolls baked together in a round pan.

April 11
CHEESE FONDUE DAY

Cheese fondue initially started as a way for Swiss villagers to reuse stale bread and dried cheese during the winter months. They'd melt the cheese with wines and herbs and then dip the bread into the gooey deliciousness to soften it. Americans were introduced to fondue during the 1964 New York World's Fair, and by the 1970s, a fondue set was a must-have on many wedding registries.

April 12
GRILLED CHEESE SANDWICH DAY

Prior to the 1960s, our version of the classic grilled cheese sandwich was slightly different. Known as "toasted cheese" or "melted cheese," the early versions of this comfort food became popular in the 1920s and consisted of grated cheese melted on top of a slice of bread. It was served open-faced. The recipe oposite is a fancy twist on one of America's favorite sandwiches.

Tiny Grilled Cheese Bites

Makes 12 mini sandwiches

INGREDIENTS

1 long French baguette, sliced into
  24 slices (each approximately
  ¼-inch-thick)
1 cup grated aged Cheddar cheese
1 cup sliced sautéed mushrooms
½ cup sliced sundried tomatoes
2 cups baby arugula
½ cup fresh basil leaves (optional)
Red pepper flakes
Kosher salt and freshly ground black
  pepper
3–4 tablespoons butter

DIRECTIONS

1. Arrange 12 slices of baguette on a dry work surface. Top with cheese, mushrooms, sundried tomatoes, arugula, and fresh basil, if using. Sprinkle with a pinch of red pepper flakes, salt, and black pepper. Top with 12 more baguette slices, making sandwiches.

2. In a large skillet over medium-low heat, melt 1½ tablespoons butter. In batches of 5 or 6, cook the sandwiches until cheese starts to melt and the outside of the sandwiches gets browned and crispy, about 3 to 4 minutes per side. Repeat with remaining butter and sandwiches.

April 13
PEACH COBBLER DAY

Cobblers harken back to the early American colonists, who, in the quest to make the beloved puddings they missed from back home, made do with a substitute dish that utilized the ingredients and cooking equipment available to them in the New World. The basic ingredients consist of fruit and a type of crust or crumb topping. The term "cobbler" is thought to derive from the "cobbled-together" appearance of the dessert. Peach cobbler was developed by the Georgia Peach Council in the 1950s as a marketing tool to sell canned peaches. To serve peach cobbler in a traditional Southern manner, be sure to add a dollop of vanilla ice cream!

April 14
PECAN DAY

The word "pecan" comes from an Algonquian word that means a nut that requires a stone to crack it. That's because pecans, like almonds and walnuts, are actually drupes, which are fruits that contain a fleshy outside with the seed—the "nut" that we eat—inside the pit. Because pecan trees are native to North America, the United States produces 80 percent of the world's pecans.

FUN FOOD FACT
The pecan became Texas' state tree in 1919.

April 15
GLAZED HAM DAY

Commonly served on Christmas and Easter, glazed hams are a holiday tradition in many American households. Ham is made by salting, smoking, or wet-curing the hind-leg section of a pig to preserve the meat. If a ham is processed with a wet brine and smoked, it is called a "city ham"; if it is dry cured and then aged, it is called a "country" ham.

April 16
EGGS BENEDICT DAY

With its decadent hollandaise sauce, eggs Benedict has been a brunch mainstay since the 1860s when Delmonico's restaurant in New York City claims to have first created it. There are conflicting accounts, however, concerning its invention. Another claim is that a chef from the Waldorf Hotel in New York City became inspired by a hungover patron who requested "some buttered toast, crisp bacon, two poached eggs, and a hooker of Hollandaise sauce." The chef then swapped in Canadian bacon and an English muffin for the customary bacon and toast. Regardless of its creator, we can all agree that everything tastes better with some hollandaise sauce!

FUN FOOD FACT

A variation known as Eggs Trivette adds Creole mustard to the hollandaise sauce and is topped with leftover crawfish tails.

Classic Eggs Benedict

Makes 4 servings

INGREDIENTS

Hollandaise
4 large egg yolks
2 tablespoons lemon juice
½ cup (1 stick) unsalted butter
½ teaspoon kosher salt

Eggs Benedict
8 slices Canadian bacon
4 English muffins
1 tablespoon white vinegar
8 large eggs

DIRECTIONS

1. To make the hollandaise sauce: Place the egg yolks and lemon juice in a blender and pulse until blended, 3 to 4 times.

2. In a small saucepan over low heat, melt the butter until warm but not boiling.

3. With the blender running, pour the butter into the egg yolk mixture and blend for about 2 minutes, or until thick and creamy. Season with salt and keep warm.

4. To make the eggs: In a large skillet over medium heat, brown the Canadian bacon, about 1 to 2 minutes per side; keep warm.

5. Split the English muffins, toast, and keep warm.

6. Fill a large skillet half full with water. Bring to boil, then reduce heat to low and simmer. Stir in the vinegar.

7. Break one egg into a small bowl and then slide it into the water. Repeat with the remaining eggs. Try to not let the eggs touch each other. Simmer the eggs uncovered for 3 to 5 minutes, just until eggs are soft cooked.

8. Remove eggs to a paper towel–lined plate with a slotted spoon.

9. To serve, place 2 halves of English muffin on each plate, top with Canadian bacon, then poached egg, then hollandaise sauce. Season with salt and pepper. Serve immediately.

April 17
CHEESE BALL DAY

A throwback to 1950s-style entertaining, cheese balls are making a comeback. One of the first recipes for this mid-century cocktail-hour hors d'oeuvre comes from the 1944 cookbook *Food of My Friends* by Virginia Safford. Cheese logs, although they are a different shape, are also considered a cheese ball.

FUN FOOD FACT
Baptist elder John Leland of Massachusetts created a massive, 1,234-pound cheese ball known as the Cheshire Mammoth Cheese and transported it by sleigh all the way to the White House in Washington, D.C., presenting it in 1802 to Thomas Jefferson as a product of voluntary and free labor, "without the assistance of a single slave."

April 18

ANIMAL CRACKERS DAY

Conjuring fond memories from our childhoods, animal crackers are a rite of passage for many American children. However, the history behind these treats begins in England in the late 1800s, when "biscuits," the British term for cookies, were made into animal shapes. The popular shapes soon made their way across the pond, and in 1871, Stauffer's Biscuit Company in York, Pennsylvania, became one of the first companies to produce the fun shapes. In 1902, the National Biscuit Company (today Nabisco) officially changed the name to Barnum's Animals Crackers and designed the packaging using the Barnum and Bailey Circus theme. During the Christmas season of the same year, a string was attached to the boxes so consumers could use them as decorations on their Christmas trees.

April 19

RICE BALL DAY

There are many different kinds of rice balls around the world, including *onigiri* from Japan, *arancini* from Italy, and *zongzi* from China. A popular Japanese quick lunch, onigiri contain salty or sour fillings wrapped in seaweed. The most common arancini rice ball is the Sicilian variety, which is stuffed with meat, tomato sauce, and mozzarella. Chinese zongzi rice balls are stuffed with different fillings, wrapped in bamboo leaves, and then steamed or boiled.

FUN FOOD FACT

Rice balls known as pinda, *which often include ghee and sesame seeds, are presented as offerings to the soul of the dead for twelve days following cremation as part of the Hindu funeral rite.*

April 20

PINEAPPLE UPSIDE-DOWN CAKE DAY

{ *A scene from a Hawaiian pineapple plantation, ca. 1910–25.*

As far back as the Middle Ages, people were cooking cakes in cast-iron pans and then flipping them over when finished. At the end of the nineteenth century, canned pineapples became readily available to Americans, and James Dole, founder of the Hawaiian Pineapple Company (later to be incorporated as the Dole Food Company), invested in a machine to slice pineapple rings. Recipes featuring the once-exotic fruit soon took off. In 1925, Dole hosted a cooking competition, and the Upside-Down Pineapple Cake was among the many pineapple recipes submitted, which became an immediate success.

Pineapple Upside-Down Muffins

Makes 12 muffins

INGREDIENTS

¼ cup (½ stick) salted butter, melted

¾ cup packed light brown sugar

2 (8-ounce) cans pineapple slices in juice, drained and juice reserved

12 maraschino cherries

1 (18.25-ounce) box white cake mix

1 tablespoon cinnamon

½ cup pineapple juice

½ cup vegetable oil

¼ cup bourbon

3 large eggs

DIRECTIONS

1. Preheat the oven to 350°F. Place 1 teaspoon melted butter in each of 12 large muffin cups. Top with 1 tablespoon brown sugar and 1 pineapple slice per cup; place 1 cherry into the center of each pineapple slice.

2. In a large bowl with a handheld mixer on low speed, beat cake mix, cinnamon, pineapple juice, oil, bourbon, and eggs until moistened. Increase heat to high speed and beat 2 minutes or until well combined and creamy.

3. Divide the batter evenly among the muffin cups. Transfer to the oven and bake for 30 to 35 minutes, or until golden brown. Cool muffins in cups for 10 minutes.

4. Place cookie sheet upside down over the muffin pan and turn over. Remove pan and serve.

April 21

CHOCOLATE-COVERED CASHEWS DAY

The cashew is actually a seed, not a nut, because it grows out of a fruit, called a drupe, which grows out of the edible cashew apple fruit. Poison ivy, cashews, mangoes, and pistachios are all part of the same plant family, *Anacardiaceae*. A toxic resin surrounds the cashew nut when it is still in its shell; therefore, cashews must always be roasted, boiled, or steamed before being eaten.

FUN FOOD FACT
The pulp of the cashew apple can be made into a sweet but very astringent juice, in addition to being fermented and distilled to create alcoholic spirits like feni, which is created exclusively in Goa, India.

April 22

JELLY BEAN DAY

Most people know that President Ronald Reagan was a huge fan of jelly beans, but what is a bit less well known is their origin. By the end of the nineteenth century, jelly beans were common and popular. The first official mention is in a 1905 *Chicago Daily News* advertisement that boasted they were sold by weight. Also during this time, the word "jelly bean" was often used to describe a man with little substance. By the 1930s, it is believed that jelly beans became associated with Easter due to their egglike shape.

April 23
PICNIC DAY

American picnics, as we know them today, became popular during the middle of the nineteenth century. The first picnic tables were used in the late 1800s and were often found in public gathering places.

{ *A family picnic, ca. 1950s.*

April 24

PIGS-IN-A-BLANKET DAY

Like all things from yesteryear, this kitschy appetizer is making a comeback . . . in some circles, at least. First appearing in Betty Crocker's *Cooking for Kids* in 1957, pigs-in-a-blanket—mini hot dogs encased in a biscuit dough—are sure to produce a smile on almost every partygoer's face. Interestingly, the first pigs-in-a-blanket date to the late 1800s and refer to oysters wrapped in bacon.

FUN FOOD FACT

In the United Kingdom, pigs-in-a-blanket are often served with turkey for Christmas dinner, alongside "devils on horseback"—prunes wrapped in bacon.

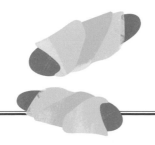

April 25
ZUCCHINI BREAD DAY

Zucchini are a type of squash that was cultivated in northern Italy at the end of the nineteenth century. Squash, however, are indigenous to Mexico and northern South America. In Italian, *zucchini* is the plural form of *zucchino*, which means "tiny squash." Zucchini became popular in the United States during the 1920s, when Italian immigrants brought them to the mainstream.

FUN FOOD FACTS

In Turkish cuisine, pancakes of shredded zucchini, flour, and eggs known as mücver *are fried in olive oil and served with a sauce of yogurt, garlic, cucumber, mint, and dill called tzatziki.*

A fully mature zucchini can be as large as a baseball bat.

The term marrow (French: courgette*) is preferred by several countries, including Great Britain, South Africa, and New Zealand.*

April 26
PRETZEL DAY

The owner of Lititz Springs Pretzel Company, Lewis C. Haines (background), in 1942, unloads a tray of pretzels that has arrived from a dumbwaiter from the baking room below. His son, Bob (foreground), weighs them and packs them in cans. Lititz was the first town in America where pretzels were made.

Pretzels have been around for a long time, but their origins are a bit murky, to say the least. Some historians think Italian (others say German) monks created them—from just salt, flour, and water— during the seventh century as treats for their students. The word "pretzel" comes from the German *bretzel*, which may come from the Latin *bracellae*, meaning "little arms." The Pennsylvania Dutch (German-speaking immigrants) are credited with bringing their pretzel-making skills to the Philadelphia region when they first settled there. One of the first companies to produce pretzels was Lititz Springs Pretzel Company in Lititz, Pennsylvania, which started in 1861. Today, soft pretzels are synonymous with Philadelphians, who consume twelve times as many pretzels per year as other Americans.

Pigs-in-a-Pretzel Blanket

Makes about 25 to 30

INGREDIENTS

1 (13.8-ounce can) pizza dough
1 (16-ounce) package cocktail
 sausages
3 tablespoons salt
½ stick butter, melted
Flaked or coarse salt, for garnish
Whole grain mustard, optional

DIRECTIONS

1. Preheat the oven to 350°F. Line a baking sheet with parchment paper; set aside.

2. Cut the pizza dough in small strips, matching the number of cocktail sausages, approximately 25 to 30. Wrap the sausages in strips of dough until covered.

3. In a large pot, bring 6 to 8 cups of water to a boil. Add the 3 tablespoons salt.

4. Carefully drop the wrapped sausages into the water and boil for 1 to 1½ minutes; remove with a slotted spoon and drain on a paper towel–lined plate.

5. Arrange sausages on the prepared baking sheet. Transfer to the oven and bake for 8 to 10 minutes, or until golden brown.

6. Remove the sausages from the oven and brush with butter. Sprinkle with salt and serve warm with whole grain mustard.

April 27
PRIME RIB DAY

Also known as a standing rib roast, prime rib is the quintessential fancy dish to serve on those extra-special occasions. It's called "standing" because the cut comes from the rib section of the beef; the rib bones act as a natural rack when cooking the meat. Whether rare, medium, or well-done, prime rib is a classic!

April 28
BLUEBERRY PIE DAY

Blueberries are native to North America and are one of the very few foods that is naturally blue. First consumed by American settlers, blueberry pie is a New England summertime favorite. The earliest known recipe of pie incorporating blueberries appeared in Maria Parloa's *Appledore Cook Book*, published in 1872. In Europe, these pies are prepared with bilberries, which are very similar to blueberries in appearance and taste.

FUN FOOD FACT

During Colonial times, the early settlers boiled blueberries in milk to make gray paint.

April 29
SHRIMP SCAMPI DAY

Scampi is the Italian plural of *scampo*, which refers to the species *Nephrops norvegicus*. Scampi, which look like crawfish, are also called langoustines, Norway lobsters, and Dublin Bay prawns. When Italian-American immigrants came to the United States, they substituted shrimp for the lesser-known scampi as the main ingredient. Although there are many culinary interpretations of shrimp scampi—some with tomato sauces, others with just oil, garlic, and white wine—each one is not only valid but also delicious!

April 30
RAISIN DAY

Raisins are dried grapes and have been cultivated for thousands of years. It is believed the Egyptians and Phoenicians introduced raisins to Europeans. Medium- and light-brown raisins are mechanically dehydrated to obtain their color while golden raisins are treated with sulfur dioxide.

FUN FOOD FACT

In French, raisin *means "grape," while a dried grape is called a* raisin sec.

MAY

Food Celebrations This Month

National Barbecue Month

National Loaded Potato Month

National Chocolate Custard Month

National Egg Month

National Hamburger Month

National Salad Month

National Salsa Month

National Strawberry Month

National Raisin Week (May 1–7)

National Herb Week (May 3–9)

National Homebrew Day (First Saturday in May)

American Craft Beer Week (The week of the third Monday of May)

May 1
SALSA DAY

Prior to Spanish rule in Mexico, the Aztecs were making salsa from tomatoes, chiles, and squash. Salsa was documented by Franciscan friar Bernardino de Sahagún, who, from 1545 until his death in 1590, studied and collected information about the Aztec culture, language, food, and customs in his twelve-book series known as the *Florentine Codex*.

FUN FOOD FACTS

The Maya civilization created salsas using mortar and pestle, which is still used for this purpose today.

Salsa verde *(green sauce) is typically made with cooked tomatillos and chili pepper in Mexican cuisine, and with herbs such as parsley in Italian cuisine.*

May 2
CHOCOLATE TRUFFLE DAY

Whether French, Swiss, Belgian, or even Californian, truffles are a very simple treat that packs a lot of flavor into a little bite. The main feature is the ganache, which contains cream mixed with melted chocolate and other flavors, such as liquors. The ganache is then coated with nuts, spices, or—traditionally—cocoa. They are called "truffles" because they resemble the fungus truffle.

May 3
RASPBERRY POPOVER DAY

Although similar to its British cousin, the Yorkshire pudding, an American popover uses butter instead of pan drippings for fat. The name popover comes from the fact that popovers "pop out" of the baking tins while they are cooking. The first written mention of a popover appears in M. N. Henderson's 1876 cookbook *Practical Cooking*.

Raspberry Popovers

Makes 12 popovers

INGREDIENTS

3 eggs

1½ cups 2% milk

1 teaspoon vanilla extract

1½ tablespoons coconut sugar

2 teaspoons chopped candied ginger

Pinch kosher salt

1½ tablespoons unsalted butter, melted

1½ cups all-purpose flour

1 cup raspberries, rinsed and patted dry

DIRECTIONS

1. Preheat the oven to 425°F. In a large bowl, blend the eggs, milk, vanilla, coconut sugar, ginger, salt, and melted butter. Add the flour and whisk until combined. Set aside.

2. Place the popover pan in the oven and heat the pan for about 10 minutes. Carefully remove the pan from the oven and spray it generously with nonstick cooking spray.

3. Fill each well about three-quarters full with batter. Top with 7 to 8 raspberries.

4. Transfer the pan to the oven and bake the popovers for 20 minutes.

5. Reduce the oven temperature to 350°F and continue baking for an additional 20 to 25 minutes.

6. After 20 minutes check the popovers.

7. Insert a sharp paring knife into each one to release the steam. Popovers are done when the knife comes out clean.

8. Let the popovers cool until cool enough to touch.

May 4
HOAGIE DAY

In some regions, lunchmeat-laden sandwiches are called heros, grinders, and subs, while in other cities they're called po' boys or Dagwoods. In Philadelphia, however, they are only known as hoagies (pronounced ʻhō-gē) and they have been the official sandwich of Philadelphia since 1992. There are numerous sources concerning how the sandwich received its name, but a common thread centers around Hog Island, which housed a naval shipyard where many Italian immigrants worked and ate the sandwiches that became known as "hoagies" for lunch.

May 5
ENCHILADA DAY

Enchiladas come in countless varieties, but they're essentially soft corn tortillas filled with fish, steak, pork, or vegetables and topped with a sauce, cheese, or sour cream. Enchiladas were a common food for the Mayans in the Yucatan Peninsula when the Spanish conquistadores arrived. One of the first documented recipes comes from the cookbook *El Cocinero Mexicano* (*The Mexican Chef*) in 1831.

May 6
CRÊPES SUZETTE DAY

Crêpes have been a beloved French dish since the beginning of the twelfth century, when buckwheat was introduced to the Brittany region. Crêpes are made by spreading a thin batter onto a hot griddle, cooking each side until light golden brown, and then filling the pancake with sweet or savory ingredients. One of the most popular sweet variations is crêpes suzette, which are crêpes topped with a sauce of orange, sugar, and liqueur (commonly Grand Marnier) followed by a flambé of brandy.

May 7
ROAST LEG OF LAMB DAY

There are different terms for meat from a sheep: lamb comes from a sheep younger than one year, hogget from a sheep older than one year, and mutton from an adult sheep.

May 8
COLA DAY

Pepsi or Coke . . . the always-controversial preference question. The one true constant is that both camps are ardent fans of their favorite. Coca-Cola was invented in 1886 by Atlanta pharmacist Dr. John Stith Pemberton, who marketed his syrup as a health aid for common ailments like headaches and indigestion. Meanwhile, pharmacist Caleb Bradham, of New Bern, North Carolina, began selling his own cola-based elixir in 1893 under the name Brad's Drink; it was renamed Pepsi-Cola in 1898.

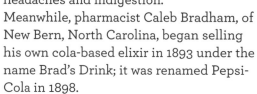

May 9
SHRIMP DAY

Not only is shrimp a very versatile ingredient, it also has very few calories, with a medium-sized shrimp containing only seven calories. Brown-colored shrimp come from the Gulf of Mexico and prefer warm water; white shrimp enjoy muddy water and are found along the Atlantic and Gulf coasts; pink shrimp, often considered the tastiest, are available from the Chesapeake Bay to the Florida Keys; tiger shrimp are abundant in Asia; and rock shrimp thrive in cold water along the Atlantic coast.

Drunken Coconut Shrimp

Makes 4 servings

INGREDIENTS

1 pound raw large shrimp, peeled and
    deveined (about 2 dozen)
Ice water, enough to cover the shrimp
1 teaspoon coarse salt
1 cup panko breadcrumbs
1 cup shredded unsweetened coconut
¾ cup brown rice flour
½ teaspoon baking powder
½ teaspoon salt
1 medium egg
6 ounces light beer
4 cups vegetable oil

DIRECTIONS

1. Place the shrimp in the ice water, then add the salt. Soak for
   15 minutes.

2. In a large stock pot, bring the oil to 350°F over medium-high heat.

3. Meanwhile, in a medium bowl, mix together the panko and
   shredded coconut. Set aside.

4. In another medium bowl, combine the flour, baking powder, salt,
   egg, and beer; whisk until combined.

5. Dip the shrimp in the beer batter and then coat with the
   panko mixture.

6. Deep-fry the shrimp for 2 to 3 minutes or until golden brown.
   Drain on paper towels and serve immediately.

May 10

LIVER AND ONIONS DAY

With roots in English cooking, liver and onions was, for generations, a common dish and a classic diner platter. The sautéed onions cut the liver's metallic taste. While it's no longer as common in the United States as in years past, it continues to be a popular dish in South America and Europe.

FUN FOOD FACT

While the much reviled dish is a great source of iron and both A and B vitamins, liver is very high in cholesterol and not a safe bet for pregnant women.

May 11

"EAT WHAT YOU WANT" DAY

Today, we celebrate you and whatever food you enjoy the most. Leave dieting, calorie counting, and feeling guilty to the remaining 364 days and simply relish in your food pleasure . . . no judgment today!

May 12
NUTTY FUDGE DAY

Contrary to popular belief, chocolate is not an essential ingredient for fudge, yet it's considered a chocolate product in the United States and Canada. A common story is that fudge was created by chance by a cook who was attempting to make caramels and the sugar accidentally crystalized, hence the expression "to fudge something."

FUN FOOD FACT

Pecans and walnuts are the most common additions to nutty fudge recipes.

May 13
HUMMUS DAY

Stemming from the Arabic word for "chickpea," hummus is an extremely popular dish in Israel and the rest of the Middle East. Usually made with tahini (sesame seed paste), lemon juice, olive oil, salt, and garlic—with countless variations in each country—hummus's exact origins are unknown; however, what is known is that chickpeas (aka garbanzo beans) have been around for thousands of years. Here in the United States, hummus has only become mainstream within the past fifteen years.

May 14
BUTTERMILK BISCUIT DAY

Traditional buttermilk is the byproduct of churning butter from cream; cultured buttermilk, which is common in supermarket aisles, is pasteurized skim or low-fat milk that has been fermented. Buttermilk was all the rage in the 1920s, when it was known as a health food and became commercially available. A staple of Southern cooking, buttermilk biscuits continue to be the star of many sweet and savory meals.

May 15
CHOCOLATE CHIP DAY

Nestlé Toll House Semi-Sweet Morsels is one of the most popular brands of chocolate chips. It was first sold in 1939, after Ruth Wakefield, the owner of Toll House Inn in Whitman, Massachusetts, used pieces of Nestlé semi-sweet chocolate in her now-famous Toll House chocolate chip cookie recipe. They are still one of America's most favorite foods and are constantly incorporated into many foods, like Ben & Jerry's Chocolate Chip Cookie Dough ice cream, which debuted in 1984 and is their number-one seller.

FUN FOOD FACT
Chocolate chips were originally created using semisweet chocolate, but now countless varieties are available, including butterscotch, white chocolate, and even mint chocolate.

May 16
BARBECUE DAY

{ *A man and woman barbecuing in the backyard, ca. 1955–65.*

W hatever style you prefer, whether it's the big hitters like Texas, Memphis, Kansas City, and North Carolina, or simply whatever you cook in your own backyard, barbecue is as American as apple pie and, for many, it conjures warm memories of summer get-togethers. Some suggest the word "barbecue" comes from the Spanish word *barbacoa*, which Spanish explorers to the Caribbean used to describe Native Americans' style of cooking. Get out a grill, pick a meat, and get the fire started to celebrate everything barbecue-related today!

May 17
CHERRY COBBLER DAY

Cobbler most likely gets its name from the way the dessert appears, "cobbled together." Interesting, cherries are part of the same family as roses and are believed to have originated in Giresun, Turkey. They came to North America via the Dutch settlers in New York City.

FUN FOOD FACT

Early English settlers in the American colonies did not have the proper ingredients or cooking equipment for traditional foods like suet pudding, so they stewed fruits like cherries and covered them with uncooked biscuits that lent a cobblestone-like appearance to their improvised dessert.

Cherry Cobbler

Makes 8 to 10 servings

INGREDIENTS

Nonstick cooking spray
1 (21-ounce) can cherry pie filling
1½ cups sugar
½ cup (1 stick) butter
1 cup all-purpose flour
2 egg whites
1 cup whole milk
1 teaspoon vanilla extract
Cinnamon, for garnish

DIRECTIONS

1. Preheat the oven to 350°F. Spray an 8 × 8-inch pan with nonstick cooking spray and set aside.

2. In a medium bowl, mix the cherry pie filling with ½ cup sugar.

3. In a small bowl, melt the butter in the microwave for about 45 seconds. Set aside.

4. In a large mixing bowl, whisk the flour, 1 cup sugar, egg whites, milk, and vanilla until smooth.

5. Whisk the melted butter into the batter. Pour the batter into the prepared pan.

6. Evenly spoon the pie filling mixture over the batter. (The batter should rise and envelop the cherries during the baking process.) Transfer the pan to the preheated oven and bake for 1 hour.

7. After removing the cobbler from the oven, sprinkle it with cinnamon and serve.

May 18
CHEESE SOUFFLÉ DAY

Instilling fear in many a cook, soufflés are the quintessential dish of haute cuisine. Made with egg whites and yolks, soufflés can be both savory and sweet. Although the origins of the soufflé are disputed, one of the first mentions of this impressive-looking dish comes from Vincent de la Chapelle, a French cook in the early eighteenth century. The name stems from the French verb *souffler*, which means "to breathe" or "to puff."

May 19
DEVIL'S FOOD CAKE DAY

Much debate swirls around how this dense cake became known as devil's food. Some argue that the name comes from the fact that baking soda mixed with cocoa power creates a reddish color, while others attribute the name to early recipes that called for beets to give the cake sweetness and moisture. Regardless of which camp one belongs to, many believe the earliest published recipe called "Devil's Food" appeared in *Mrs. Rorer's New Cook Book* in 1902.

FUN FOOD FACT
A similar Southern favorite, red velvet cake, is topped with cream cheese frosting.

May 20
QUICHE LORRAINE DAY

Considered a classic French dish, quiche Lorraine has a history that begins in the medieval kingdom of Lothringen in Germany (later named Lorraine by the French). The traditional ingredients include bacon, eggs, and crème fraîche—cheese was added in later versions—that are mixed into a custard and then baked in an open piecrust. Due to rationing during World War II, quiche Lorraine became a popular dish in England, and after the war, it crossed the pond and became a hit in the United States in the 1950s.

May 21
STRAWBERRIES & CREAM DAY

{ *A worker picking strawberries in a field near Hammond, Louisiana, 1939.*

Strawberries were eaten by the Native Americans, who called them "heart-seed berries," before the first European settlers arrived in North America. An interesting fact is that the average strawberry contains two hundred seeds on its surface and is the only fruit to have seeds on the outside.

FUN FOOD FACT

Because strawberries have had a long association with love, a traditional French custom was to serve newlyweds a bowl of strawberry soup.

May 22
VANILLA PUDDING DAY

First developed during the Middle Ages in Europe, pudding has progressed over the centuries and is more related to custard than English puddings. Originally, a dish for the wealthy called *blancmange*, or "white dish," the first puddings were both savory—with chicken, fish, and meat—and sweet. Later, during the 1840s, cornstarch and arrowroot were added to thicken the recipe and the modern vanilla pudding was born. In the 1940s, the first instant varieties started to appear on the market.

{ *A 1918 poster advertising the "wholesome, nutritious foods from corn," one of which is pudding.*

May 23
TAFFY DAY

Since 1880, salt water taffies have been a New Jersey Shore treat for generations of beachgoers. Contrary to popular belief, salt water taffy is not made with salt water but, rather, very simple ingredients that are pulled with a machine to aerate the taffy. Prior to the invention of the machine, "candy pull" parties were a popular pastime in the nineteenth century, especially among children.

May 24
ESCARGOT DAY

Let's admit it, *escargot*, or snails, is not on the list of typical dishes for most Americans, but in Europe the dish has been around for centuries and is considered a delicacy. In fact, the first known cookbook, a collection of ancient Roman recipes called *Apicus*, has instructions for preparing snails.

FUN FOOD FACT
The science of growing snails is called heliciculture.

May 25
WINE DAY

Where would the world be without wine? The earliest known consumption of wine dates to 7000 B.C. in China. The oldest wine bottle dates to 325 A.D. from the grave of a Roman nobleman's tomb and is housed in the Historical Museum of the Palatinate in Speyer, Germany.

FUN FOOD FACT

Women are better wine tasters than men.

May 26
BLUEBERRY CHEESECAKE DAY

It is believed that the precursor to cheesecake was invented in ancient Greece, yet the relatively modern invention of cream cheese in 1872 by William Lawrence from Chester, New York—while attempting to make a French Neufchâtel—is the star ingredient in today's recipes. In 1880, Philadelphia Brand Cream Cheese began to be distributed by Alvah Reynolds, which would eventually merge with Kraft Foods in 1928.

A worker picking blueberries near Little Fork, Minnesota, 1937.

May 27
GRAPE POPSICLE DAY

The origin of Popsicles is a true testament to the fact that one is never too young to be a great inventor. In 1905, an eleven-year-old boy named Frank Epperson left a cup full of water, powdered soda, and a stick outside on his porch in San Francisco. The next day he had a frozen treat. Twenty years later, Frank became a partner with the Joe Lowe Company in New York, which began to distribute the ices around the country. Frank named his flavored ices "Epsicle," but his children, who called them "Pop's 'sicle," urged him to rename them Popsicle. Although cherry is the most popular flavor, feel free to celebrate all flavors today, like grape!

May 28
BRISKET DAY

Brisket is an extremely popular dish in Jewish cooking. It's served on the Sabbath, as well as on many holidays, such as Rosh Hashanah and Passover. The brisket comes from the lower chest of cattle, which has a high amount of collagen fibers, making it a tough cut that requires a long cooking time. In Texas, brisket is the quintessential cut of meat for classic Texan barbecue.

Slow-Cooker BBQ Brisket

Makes 8 servings

INGREDIENTS

¼ cup paprika

1 tablespoon chili powder

1 tablespoon ground cumin

1 tablespoon ground nutmeg

1 tablespoon packed dark brown
    sugar

1 tablespoon kosher salt, plus more
    as needed

1 teaspoon cayenne pepper

2 teaspoons onion powder

2 teaspoons freshly ground black
    pepper

1 (5- to 7-pound) beef brisket

1½ cups barbecue sauce (your choice
    of brand)

DIRECTIONS

1. In a medium bowl, mix together all of the spices.

2. Place the brisket on a cutting board and cut it in half widthwise.

3. Evenly coat it with the spice rub and place the 2 brisket pieces and the barbecue sauce in the slow cooker. Cover and cook on low until fork-tender, about 10 hours.

4. Transfer the brisket to a clean cutting board.

5. Pour the sauce drippings from the slow cooker into a medium heatproof bowl and set aside.

6. Remove the excess fat from the brisket and discard. Shred the meat with 2 forks.

7. With a spoon, skim and discard the fat from the surface of the drippings. Return the sauce and the shredded meat to the slow cooker and stir gently to combine. Season with salt and pepper as needed and serve.

May 29
BISCUIT DAY

A type of quick bread, the biscuit has been around for centuries in slightly different forms. What Americans today consider biscuits dates to the pre–Civil War era, when Southern cooks devised a simple bread without yeast or a leavening agent to accompany their dishes. Today, there are numerous variations—but the classic will always be the buttermilk biscuit.

{ *A woman making biscuits for dinner near Tallyho, Granville County, North Carolina, 1939.*

May 30
MINT JULEP DAY

Synonymous with the Kentucky Derby since 1938, mint juleps have a long history in the South. While mint juleps were most likely first mixed with rye whiskey or rum, bourbon whiskey became the spirit of choice. The term "julep" was long associated with a syrup drink mixed with medicine. Early Virginians used to drink mint juleps in pewter or silver cups.

May 31
MACAROON DAY

Because there is no leavening agent in macaroons, these delicious sweets are a popular dish for Passover. By the late 1800s, coconut became readily available, and soon all kinds of recipes were appearing with this exotic new ingredient, one of which was macaroons. A macaroon recipe was featured in Esther Levy's *Jewish Cookery Book* in 1871, which was the first Jewish-American cookbook.

FUN FOOD FACT
Coconut macaroons are called congolais *in France, where the* macaron *(spelled with one "o") is an entirely different confectionary all together.*

Food Celebrations This Month

National Candy Month

National Dairy Month

National Fresh Fruits and Vegetables Month

National Iced Tea Month

National Papaya Month

National Doughnut Day (First Friday in June)

June 1

HAZELNUT CAKE DAY

The word "hazelnut" comes from the Anglo-Saxon word *haesel*, which means "bonnet" or "headdress," since the nut naturally looks like one. The hazelnut has been Oregon's state nut since 1989. Hazelnuts are also called filberts.

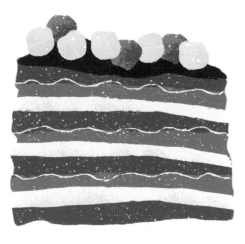

June 2

ROCKY ROAD DAY

Like many conflicting stories of food origins, today's celebratory ice cream flavor claims a couple of inventors. One claim comes from William Dreyer and Joseph Edy, cofounders of Edy's Grand Ice Cream (later to be marketed as Dreyer's in the West and Edy's in the East and Midwest after William and Joseph parted ways). In 1929, in Oakland, California, Dreyer and Edy decided to add marshmallows and almonds to chocolate ice cream. They named the invention "Rocky Road" after the 1929 stock market crash. Another claim comes from *Rigby's Reliable Candy Teacher*, 13th edition, which was published in 1920 and has a recipe for Rocky Road. The recipe is slightly different than today's version, but still contains the basic ingredients. No matter who the inventor was, can anything really taste bad with chocolate?

June 3
EGG DAY

We Americans love our eggs, with most people eating an average of 250 a year. One way to tell the difference between an old and fresh egg is to place it in a bowl of water. If the eggs sinks, it's fresh; if it floats, it's not. Depending the hen's breed, she will lay different-colored eggs, such as blue, white, brown, and reddish-green.

{ *A woman jumping out of an egg, ca. 1920s.*

FUN FOOD FACTS

In 2013, the six-billion-plus population of laying hens produced 68.3 million metric tons of eggs worldwide, with China as the top producer by far.

Before chickens arrived in ancient Greece around 800 B.C., the quail was their primary source of eggs.

June 4
CHEESE DAY

Although cheesemaking dates back to the earliest civilizations, 8000 to 3000 B.C. by some accounts, the ancient Greeks and Romans were the ones who perfected the art, making cheese an extremely valuable item. Each region developed its unique flavor and process depending on its available resources and climate. After the Roman Empire, monks began to create today's classic and traditional cheese varieties. The United States is the biggest producer of cheese, but Greece and Finland top the lists for most cheese consumption.

FUN FOOD FACT
Wisconsin is the Unites States' biggest producer of cheddar cheese.

{ *Wisconsin Senator Alexander Wiley presenting Mrs. Garner a 2,200-pound cheddar cheese bust of her husband, Vice President John Garner, in celebration of Wisconsin's Diamond Jubilee Cheese Week, 1939.*

June 5
KETCHUP / CATSUP DAY

Ketchup and catsup are the same condiment, but the product (and its spelling) has an interesting history. By the end of the seventeenth century, British sailors began returning home from the Far East with bottles of a food condiment made from fermented fish guts and spices. They called it catchup, from the Chinese word *kôechiap*. During the 1700 and 1800s, the English experimented with the recipe and altered it, and soon variations with anchovies, tomatoes, and vinegar appeared. Early cookbooks from the 1800s call it catsup, as did H. J. Heinz Company, which first started producing its famous table sauce in 1876; however, they switched the name to ketchup in the 1880s, and that spelling has been preferred.

June 6
GINGERBREAD DAY

Gingerbread comes in many forms, from festive, holiday-decorated women and men cookies to spicy cakes. While we don't know much about the history of gingerbread, we do know that gingerbread figures were very popular in medieval Europe, with stands appearing at fairs and festivals, especially in England and Germany, where gingerbread was considered a health food due to the spices. There are countless gingerbread variations, but the basic ingredients are ginger, cinnamon, cloves, and nutmeg. In the United States, molasses became a common addition, since it was much cheaper than sugar before the end of the nineteenth century.

FUN FOOD FACT

The English town of Market Drayton, which has been making gingerbread since at least the late eighteenth century, became particularly known for their version of the cookie, which is flavored with rum and lemon in addition to ginger.

June 7
CHOCOLATE ICE CREAM DAY

With references dating as far back as Alexander the Great, ice cream has been around for a very long time. Fueled by innovation, American ice cream history starts in 1777, when the first ice cream advertisement appeared in the *New York Gazette*. It was available almost exclusively to the upper classes, but that quickly changed in 1851 when Jacob Fussell, a milk distributor from Baltimore, Maryland, began to manufacture and sell affordable ice cream to the masses. The first ice cream cone recipe is attributed to Agnes Bertha Marshall and appears in the English cookbook *Mrs. A. B. Marshall's Book of Cookery* in 1888. It was called "Cornet with Cream." They became immensely popular during the 1904 World's Fair.

Two women enjoying ice cream cones in Washington Square Park in New York City, 1917, sponsored by the National League for Women's Service to benefit the Red Cross and other war relief agencies.

June 8
JELLY-FILLED DOUGHNUT DAY

Germans and German-Americans have a tradition of eating jelly doughnuts on New Year's Eve to bring good luck—beware, though, if you are celebrating in Germany, because it's a common practical joke to fill the doughnuts with mustard instead of jelly for a fun surprise! The largest doughnut on record was a jelly doughnut weighing 1.7 tons in 1993 in Utica, New York.

June 9
STRAWBERRY-RHUBARB PIE DAY

Originally from China, rhubarb was considered throughout history to be a medicinal plant with healing qualities. By the eighteenth century, it began to be used in cooking, and early recipes called for its use in stews and drinks. Today, it's most often paired with strawberry and other sweet ingredients, like sugar and honey, for pies. Remember: Never eat the leaves, cooked or raw, as they are poisonous!

{ *Two women holding a rhubarb stalk in southeastern Alaska, ca. 1900–30.*

Classic Strawberry-Rhubarb Pie

Makes 1 (9-inch) pie

INGREDIENTS

1½ cups sugar
3 tablespoons quick-cooking tapioca
¼ teaspoon kosher salt
¼ teaspoon ground nutmeg
3 cups rhubarb, cut in ½-inch pieces
1 cup sliced fresh strawberries
1 tablespoon salted butter, diced
2 premade piecrusts
1 egg, beaten
Coarse sugar

DIRECTIONS

1. Preheat the oven to 400°F. Grease a 9-inch pie plate.

2. In a large bowl, combine the sugar, tapioca, salt, and nutmeg. Add the rhubarb and strawberries, mixing to coat the fruit. Let stand about 20 minutes.

3. Line the pie plate with one of the crusts, crimping the excess on the sides. Fill it with the marinated fruit, and dot with the butter.

4. With the second piecrust, create a lattice top or just place the second crust on top and cut heat vents; seal the edges. Brush the top with egg wash and dust with coarse sugar.

5. Transfer the pie plate to the preheated oven and bake for 35 to 40 minutes or until crust is cooked through.

6. Serve with vanilla ice cream (optional).

June 10
ICED TEA DAY

Although many credit the 1904 World's Fair in Saint Louis, Missouri, with introducing iced tea to Americans, recipes for this immensely popular drink were already appearing in cookbooks in the early nineteenth century, especially in the South, where green tea was used in many early tea punches. As refrigeration improved and became more prevalent, so, too, did iced tea as a beverage option, and black tea became the leaf of choice. Today, sweet tea, which is made by steeping tea and adding lots and lots of sugar, is preferred in the South, while outside the South it is more common to find unsweetened iced tea.

June 11
GERMAN CHOCOLATE CAKE DAY

Contrary to the common misconception that German chocolate cake has German roots, this decadent chocolate, caramel, coconut, and pecan cake starts its history in 1852, when a man named Samuel German invented a dark baking chocolate called Baker's German's Sweet Chocolate for the Baker Chocolate Company, the oldest chocolate maker in the United States (now owned by General Foods). Then, in 1957, a homemaker from Dallas, Texas, submitted a cake recipe to a local newspaper and called it "German's Chocolate Cake," which became an overnight success. Over the years, German's dropped the apostrophe and "s" and the cake became known simply as German Chocolate Cake.

June 12
PEANUT BUTTER COOKIE DAY

In 1897, a *Popular Science Monthly* article recommended peanut butter as a good substitute for butter, shortening, or lard. Thanks to this article, as well as strong advocacy by George Washington Carver—an educator, scientist, and botanist from the Tuskegee Institute who believed in peanuts as a nutritious, self-sustaining food source—peanuts and peanut butter quickly gained in popularity. Peanut-based recipes started filling cookbooks and by the early 1930s, recipes for the first peanut butter cookies could be found.

June 13
CUPCAKE LOVERS' DAY

Although claims to the first cupcake recipe vary, most food historians agree that the precursors to these little cakes were called "1, 2, 3, 4 Cakes," "Number Cakes," or "Quarter Cakes," referring to the number of ingredients or "cups" of each ingredient—1 cup butter, 2 cups sugar, 3 cups flour, 4 eggs—needed to make a cake before Fannie Farmer standardized cooking measurements in the late 1890s. In 1919, Hostess introduced its "CupCake," but it wouldn't be until 1950 that the signature squiggly lines would appear on top, differentiating Hostess's product from its competitors'. Cupcakes took the food scene by storm in the early 2000s, with stores and bakeries nationwide dedicated solely to making these easy-to-eat snacks.

June 14
STRAWBERRY SHORTCAKE DAY

Due to the relatively short strawberry season in early summer, until transportation linked the various American regions, cooks had a limited time to enjoy these fresh berries, especially in the cities. By the 1850s, strawberry parties were synonymous with the coming of summer, and various strawberry-related recipes began to be circulated. Nowadays, it is common to see sponge cake, strawberries, and whipped cream as the featured ingredients in strawberry shortcake, but a true shortcake is similar to a biscuit dough, with "short" possibly referring to its relatively short height from rising when baked. Regardless of which type of shortcake you make, anything with strawberries is a winner!

Buttermilk Strawberry Shortcake

Makes 6 servings

INGREDIENTS

Shortcake
1½ cups all-purpose flour
2½ teaspoons baking powder
½ teaspoon baking soda
1½ tablespoons sugar
½ teaspoon kosher salt
1 teaspoon orange zest
½ cup (1 stick) cold salted butter, diced
½ cup buttermilk
Coarse sugar

Topping
3 cups fresh strawberries, sliced
1 tablespoon sugar
1 tablespoon orange juice
1 teaspoon orange zest
Whipped cream, for serving

DIRECTIONS

1. Preheat the oven to 425°F and line a baking sheet with parchment paper.

2. To make the shortcake: In the bowl of a food processor, combine the flour, baking powder, baking soda, sugar, salt, and orange zest. Pulse 3 to 5 times or until combined.

3. Add the cold butter and pulse a few times with a food processor (or cut in the butter by hand in a bowl using a pastry cutter) until it is like coarse crumbs. Transfer the mixture to a large bowl and stir in the buttermilk. Do not overmix.

4. Drop heaping 2 tablespoons of dough onto the prepared pan. Sprinkle with coarse sugar. Transfer to the preheated oven and bake for 15 minutes or until lightly browned. Allow to cool slightly while you prepare the topping.

5. To make the topping: In a large bowl, combine the strawberries, sugar, orange juice, and orange zest; stir well and let sit at room temperature at least 30 minutes to allow the strawberries to release their juices.

6. To serve, slice the shortcakes in half and top with strawberries and whipped cream.

June 15
LOBSTER DAY

During Colonial times, lobsters were considered a poor man's food, due to their abundant supply; in fact, some servants were so tired of eating lobster that they wrote into their contracts that their employers could only feed them lobster once a week.

{ *A large lobster brought in by a New England fishing boat at the Fulton Fish Market in New York City, 1943.*

June 16
FUDGE DAY

Considered an American invention, fudge can be a little finicky to make, as it's easy to overcook, undercook, or overstir it, altering the final result. One popular origin story has a Vassar College student from Poughkeepsie, New York, writing in an 1888 letter about a classmate's cousin making the first batch of fudge, which then became a hit at other women's colleges. Others claim it was accidently discovered by a chocolatier in Baltimore, Maryland, while making a batch of caramels. Accidental or not, one cannot "fudge" the fact that these melt-in-your-mouth morsels are truly delicious.

The Perfect Fudge

Makes 24 pieces

INGREDIENTS

Nonstick cooking spray
3 cups sugar
6 tablespoons salted butter
1 (5-ounce) can evaporated milk
1 cup semisweet chocolate chips
1 cup bittersweet chocolate chips
1 (7-ounce) jar Marshmallow Fluff
½ teaspoon kosher salt
½ cup pecans, chopped
½ cup walnuts, chopped

DIRECTIONS

1. Line a 9 x 13-inch baking pan with foil and spray with nonstick cooking spray.

2. In a double boiler, bring the sugar, butter, and evaporated milk to a rolling boil over medium heat. Stir constantly until the temperature reads 234°F on a candy thermometer, 5 to 6 minutes.

3. Remove the mixture from the heat and add the chocolate chips and marshmallow fluff. Stir until completely melted.

4. Add the salt and nuts and stir until combined.

5. Pour the mixture into the prepared pan and let cool completely.

6. Lift the foil out of the pan and cut the fudge into 2- to 3-inch squares and serve.

June 17
APPLE STRUDEL DAY

Apple strudel is most commonly associated with Austria, and the oldest known strudel recipe dates to 1696. *Strudel* means "whirlpool" in German and refers to how the pastry looks when rolled up. Many believe the technique for making apple strudel came from the Ottoman Empire, which introduced thin filo pastries, such as baklava, to Central Europe via Hungary. The most common strudel filling is apples, cinnamon, sugar, breadcrumbs, and raisins, but like all national foods, countless varieties exist.

June 18
CHEESE-MAKERS DAY

The Puritans brought their cheesemaking skills with them when they arrived in the New World, with the Massachusetts, New York, and Vermont colonies serving as dairy centers before pioneers started settling the Western states.

{ *Workers packing cheese into molds in Tillamook, Oregon, 1941.*

June 19
MARTINI DAY

Associated with the Roaring Twenties, the Streamlined Fifties, and today's various "-tini" concoctions, martinis have a long and varied history in the cocktail world and are considered by many to be king of cocktail sophistication. There is quite a bit of speculation as to where and when the first martini came from, with some accounts claiming that the 1870s Martinez Cocktail from the Occidental Hotel in San Francisco, California, was the martini precursor, while others purport the name comes from Alessandro Martini, the founder of the Italian vermouth company Martini & Rossi. What is known is that by the 1920s, the common martini contained a 2 to 1, or 1 to 1, ratio of London dry gin to dry vermouth; however, as the years progressed, the vermouth ratio greatly diminished, to today's common recipe of a dash of vermouth—a "dry" martini—with vodka replacing gin. Also popular is the "dirty martini," which adds a splash of olive juice. Regardless of the martini's origins, enjoy one today . . . responsibly, of course.

FUN FOOD FACT
American writer E. B. White referred to the martini as the "elixir of quietude."

June 20
VANILLA MILKSHAKE DAY

{ *A woman seated at a soda fountain table pouring hidden alcohol into a cup from a cane during Prohibition, 1922.*

One of America's favorite malt shop drinks, the milkshake conjures up images of a bygone era complete with jukeboxes, soda jerks, and early rock 'n' roll. Many credit Ivan "Pop" Coulson with creating the milkshake in 1922. A Walgreens employee, Coulson was constantly playing with different combinations of drinks. The early prototype to milkshakes was a "malted milk," which contained chocolate syrup, milk, and malt powder. One day, Coulson decided to add two scoops of ice cream to a malted milk . . . and the rest, as they say, is history. There are so many milkshakes variations and names—frappés, cabinets, frosted shakes, and velvets—each with its own unique recipe, that it is next to impossible to identify America's favorite flavor. Interestingly, the very first "milkshake" recipes from the late 1880s contained whiskey.

June 21
PEACHES & CREAM DAY

Originally from China, peaches were introduced to South America by Spanish explorers, and English settlers brought them to the colonies. Popular in the South, peaches and cream is a simple dessert consisting of peach slices and whipped cream that is often served in the summer, when peaches are at peak ripeness.

FUN FOOD FACT
A nectarine is a variety of peach that does not have a fuzzy skin; it is not a hybrid.

June 22
ONION RING DAY

While the exact origins of the onion ring are unknown, one of the first documented onion ring recipes appeared as a Crisco Oil advertisement in the *New York Times Magazine* in 1933. The Blooming Onion, or Onion Blossom, is a popular appetizer in many restaurants, with a Scotty's Steak House in Springfield, New Jersey, claiming to be its inventor in the 1970s.

June 23
PECAN SANDY DAY

A shortbread cookie with pecans, the pecan sandy has nebulous roots, but some believe it was influenced by Arabic cuisine, with the name most likely derived from the cookie's sandlike color.

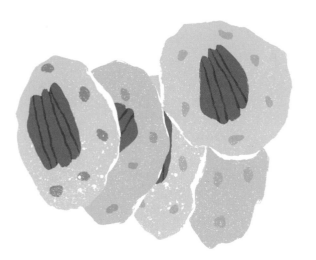

June 24
PRALINES DAY

A beautiful combination of nuts and sugar, American pralines, which are a classic New Orleans tradition, owe their roots to French pralines, which commonly used almonds. However, when French explorers arrived in the Crescent City and were met with an abundance of pecans, they switched out the starring nut and added cream, making pralines more similar to fudge. Just be sure to pronounce them "praw-lines" like a true New Orleanian.

June 25
CATFISH DAY

Catfish can be found in both freshwater and coastal regions all around the world except Antarctica. Catfish get their name from the cat-whisker-like barbels that surround their mouth and contain their taste buds. Catfish is an extremely popular dish in the southern United States and is often served breaded with cornmeal or fried.

June 26
CHOCOLATE PUDDING DAY

In 1934, General Foods (Jell-O) debuted its chocolate pudding mix and called it "Walter's Baker's Dessert," which was renamed "Pickle's Pudding" in 1936. Pudding, in general, was commonly thought to be a health food in the late-nineteenth century, so feel free to use that rationalization the next time you are snacking on a cup of chocolate pudding!

FUN FOOD FACT
Black bottom pie is an American dessert from the early to mid-1900s in which chocolate pudding is layered on a graham cracker crust, with whipped cream on top.

June 27
ORANGE BLOSSOM DAY

Due to its traditional association with good fortune, the orange blossom is a popular flower choice in wedding bouquets. Its leaves are used to make orange flower water, a common ingredient in many Mediterranean dishes.

FUN FOOD FACT
The orange blossom is Florida's state flower.

June 28
TAPIOCA PUDDING DAY

Extracted from the cassava root, which is indigenous to Brazil, tapioca is used as a thickening agent for many different foods, such as pies, gravies, soups, puddings, and bubble tea. After fermenting, washing, and pressing, cassava root is then dried and crushed into a fine white powder known as tapioca flour or instant tapioca, or it can be pressed into small or large tapioca pearls.

Traditional Tapioca Pudding

Makes *4 servings*

INGREDIENTS

½ cup small pearl tapioca
  (not instant)
2 cups whole milk
1 cup heavy cream
¼ teaspoon kosher salt
½ cup sugar
2 large eggs
1 teaspoon cinnamon
1 teaspoon vanilla extract

DIRECTIONS

1. In a medium saucepan over medium heat, combine the tapioca, milk, cream, and salt, stirring constantly while bringing to a simmer.

2. Lower the heat to simmer and cook uncovered, adding sugar gradually, until the tapioca pearls have thickened, about 5 minutes.

3. In a large bowl, beat the eggs. To avoid curdling, mix in some of the hot tapioca very slowly to equalize the temperature of the two mixtures.

4. Add the egg mixture to the saucepan. Increase the heat to medium and stir for several minutes, until it reaches the consistency of a thick pudding. Do not let the mixture boil or the pudding will curdle.

5. Remove the pudding from the heat and let cool 15 minutes. Stir in the cinnamon and vanilla.

ALMOND BUTTER-CRUNCH DAY

With a crunchy toffee base covered with nuts and/or chocolate, almond buttercrunch can be enjoyed by itself or used as a topping for ice cream. One of the oldest makers is Brown & Haley Company from Tacoma, Washington, which started in 1914 and introduced Almond Roca in 1923. Its name is said to have been derived from the Spanish word *roca*, which means "rock."

FUN FOOD FACTS

The world's largest producer of almonds is California, which has an 800,000-acre stretch of almond trees in the northern part of the state that provides 82 percent of global demand.

Although there are eight major varieties of almonds, the most popular is the nonpareil, which have a mild sweetness and a light-colored skin.

June 30
MAI TAI
DAY

In Tahitian, *maita'I* means "good," which is appropriate, as this tropical drink brings to mind Polynesian sunsets, floral printed shirts, and pretty much anything tiki related. Although it became immensely popular in the 1950s and 1960s, the mai tai is said to have been created by Victor Bergeron in 1944 at his Hinky Dink's restaurant (which later became the Trader Vic's franchise) in Oakland, California. Bergeron served the fruity cocktail to his Tahitian friends who called it "very good," and the name was born. However, rival restaurateur Donn Beach, who founded Don the Beachcomber restaurants, also claims to have invented the mai tai in 1933. Although each version is slightly different, both Victor and Don knew a "good" thing when they tasted it!

July

Food Celebrations This Month

National Baked Bean Month

National Culinary Arts Month

National Hot Dog Month

National Ice Cream Month

National Picnic Month

National Pickle Month

July 1
GINGERSNAP DAY

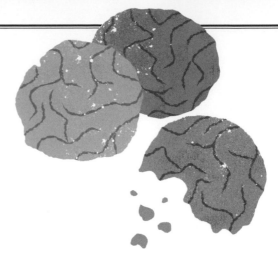

{ *Tins of Lebkuchen (cookies) probably manufactured by the German company Baren-Schmidt, ca. 1910–15.*

Gingersnaps, also called ginger biscuits or ginger nuts, can trace their origins to medieval Germany. After traders in India began exporting powdered ginger root and other spices to Europe for use in baking, thirteenth-century monks invented treats known as *Lebkuchen* that contained honey, nuts, and various spices. Beginning in the fifteenth century, harder variations of this gingerbread were cut into various shapes and decorated during the Christmas season, and a century later the first gingerbread men were served at the English court of Queen Elizabeth I. Traditionally containing inexpensive molasses in place of honey or refined sugar, gingersnaps have remained popular for centuries in Europe as well as America thanks in part to ginger's reputation for calming the stomach.

July 2
ANISETTE DAY

Anisette, an anise-flavored liqueur popular in the Mediterranean region, was first created in France by combining a neutral spirit with sugar and the oil of green anise seeds. In the fourth century B.C., Greek physician Hippocrates recommended anise for easing coughs—advice that is still heeded today. Anise also flavors licorice candy as well as the high-proof "green fairy" spirit that enchanted many famous writers: absinthe. Like other anise-based liqueurs—including pastis (France), sambuca (Italy), and ouzo (Greece)—anisette is often combined with cold water to produce a cloudy sweet-and-spicy aperitif.

July 3
CHOCOLATE WAFER DAY

In the medieval period, sovereigns consumed wafers at the end of a state meal in a ceremony representing the final grace and washing of hands. Since then, these thin, crisp pastries have taken many forms. French cannelons are essentially wafers rolled into tubes and filled with hazelnut cream, chocolate, preserves, or other fillings. Often used as decoration for ice cream, they can also be arranged in thin layers with cream filling in between. The commercial chocolate wafer got its start in 1924, when the company now known as Nabisco began selling them.

July 4
CEASAR SALAD DAY

While this ubiquitous salad may call to mind the storied Roman emperor, it was invented on July 4, 1924, by the Italian immigrant Caesar Cardini. After his restaurant in Tijuana, ran out of several ingredients during the American holiday rush, he reportedly combined leftover romaine lettuce, olive oil, egg, garlic, Parmesan, and Worcestershire sauce for several customers, tossing it with flair in front of them. The salad was popular among the Hollywood elite before it became an American restaurant staple.

{ *A cooking class making salads at the John Hay School in Chicago, Illinois, 1929.*

FUN FOOD FACT
The famous cook Julia Child claimed to have eaten a Caesar salad at Cardini's restaurant in the 1920s.

A Modern Ceasar Salad

Makes 4 to 6 servings

INGREDIENTS

2 cloves garlic, peeled

½ teaspoon kosher salt

2 tablespoons lemon juice

1½ teaspoons Worcestershire sauce

2 tablespoons anchovy paste

½ cup extra-virgin olive oil

¼ cup full-fat Greek yogurt

2 heads romaine lettuce, torn into bite-size pieces

2 cups prepared croutons

½ cup shredded Parmesan cheese

DIRECTIONS

1. In a blender, combine the garlic, salt, lemon juice, Worcestershire sauce, anchovy paste, olive oil, and yogurt. Blend on high for 1 to 2 minutes, or until smooth and well combined.

2. Transfer the dressing to a large salad bowl. Add the romaine and croutons. Toss until coated. Sprinkle with the Parmesan cheese.

July 5
APPLE TURNOVER DAY

Turnovers are flaky, buttery baked pastries created by folding dough over a filling. There are many sweet and savory varieties worldwide, including Italian calzones, Spanish empanadas, and Polish pierogis. Sweetened apples are a common filling in the English and American varieties, which became popular in the 1800s and were described in Laura Ingalls Wilder's *Little House on the Prairie* children's novels.

{ *A shipment of Missouri apples at the Saint Louis riverfront, 1923.*

July 6
FRIED CHICKEN DAY

{ *A butcher weighing a chicken for a client, ca. 1930s.*

FUN FOOD FACT
In the American South, fried chicken continues to be among the region's top choices for "Sunday dinner."

Unlike the English, who preferred to bake or boil chicken, the Scots had a tradition of deep-frying chicken in fat as far back as the Middle Ages. After Scottish immigrants introduced fried chicken to the American South, the African slaves—who were cooks in many Southern households—enriched the flavor by incorporating seasonings and spices that were absent in traditional Scottish cuisine. The earliest known written recipe for American-style fried chicken appeared in *The Art of Cookery Made Plain and Easy*, a British cookbook published in 1747. Fried chicken travels well in hot weather, so it gained favor over other foods before refrigeration became commonplace.

July 7
MACARONI DAY

The term *macaroni* refers to any dish in which pasta noodles are cooked in water or broth, but in America, macaroni is typically associated with elbow-shaped noodles served with melted cheese. Pasta and cheese casseroles were described the fourteenth-century cookbooks *Liber de Coquina* (Italy) and *Forme of Cury* (England), the latter of which referred to the dish as "makerouns," but the first modern recipe didn't appear until 1770. After returning from a trip to Paris and northern Italy, Thomas Jefferson brought home a sketch of "macaroni" noodles, which he later imported to America and presented—in pie form—at a state dinner in 1802.

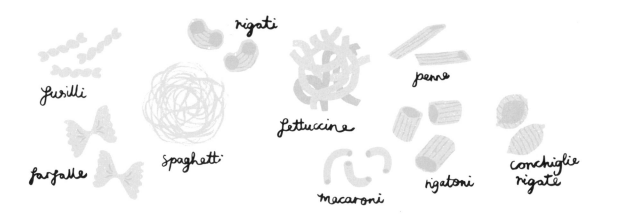

fusilli

rigati

lettuccine

penne

farfalle

spaghetti

macaroni

rigatoni

conchiglie rigate

Classic Mac & Cheese

Makes 8 servings

INGREDIENTS

Nonstick cooking spray
1 (16-ounce) box macaroni

Crispy Topping
2 tablespoons unsalted butter
1 cup Italian-seasoned panko
   breadcrumbs

Cheese Sauce
¼ cup (½ stick) salted butter
4 cloves garlic, crushed
¼ cup all-purpose flour
3½ cups 2% milk
1 cup heavy cream
1 tablespoon cornstarch
1 tablespoon cold water
Kosher salt and freshly ground black
   pepper
¾ cup shredded extra-sharp Cheddar
   cheese
1 cup grated Parmesan cheesep
½ cup shredded Gruyère cheese
½ cup shredded mozzarella cheese

DIRECTIONS

1. Preheat the oven to 375°F. Spray a 9 x 13-inch baking dish with nonstick cooking spray.

2. Cook the pasta in salted boiling water according to the package instructions. Drain and rinse with cold water.

3. To make the topping: In a medium skillet over medium heat, melt 2 tablespoons butter. Add the breadcrumbs, stir, and cook until golden brown. Transfer to a bowl and set aside.

4. To make the sauce: To the same skillet, melt the ¼ cup butter. Add the garlic and sauté until fragrant. Whisk in the flour and continue cooking while stirring for about 2 minutes.

5. Reduce the heat to low, gradually whisk in the milk and cream, and keep whisking constantly. Bring the mixture to a boil until it begins to thicken.

6. In a separate bowl, combine the cornstarch and cold water, whisking until there are no lumps. Stir the cornstarch mixture into the sauce to thicken it. Cook, whisking constantly, for 1 minute longer. Season to taste with salt and pepper.

7. Remove the sauce from the heat and add the Cheddar cheese, ¾ cup Parmesan cheese, Gruyère, and mozzarella. Stir until all of the cheese has melted. Toss the cooked pasta with the sauce until completely coated, and transfer to the prepared pan.

8. Top with the breadcrumbs and remaining ¼ cup Parmesan cheese. Transfer the pan to the preheated oven and bake for 10 minutes or until lightly browned and bubbling.

July 8
CHOCOLATE WITH ALMONDS DAY

Originating in the Middle East, the bitter variety of almond contains amygdalin—a chemical found in the seeds of peaches, apples, and other stone fruits that transforms into deadly hydrogen cyanide when crushed or chewed. Almonds are the most nutrient-dense tree nut, containing 160 calories per ounce, and they are a great source of vitamin E, magnesium, protein, and riboflavin. The Jordan almond, which has a pastel-colored candy coating, is often distributed as a wedding favor in the Mediterranean region.

FUN FOOD FACTS

In a recent survey, 70 percent of respondents across the globe said they preferred chocolate with nuts over chocolate by itself, and the most preferred nut pairing with chocolate was the almond.

The combination of dark chocolate and almonds has been promoted in recent years as a potentially heart-protective treat, owing to the antioxidant properties of cocoa and the cholesterol-lowering phytosterols in almonds.

July 9
SUGAR COOKIE DAY

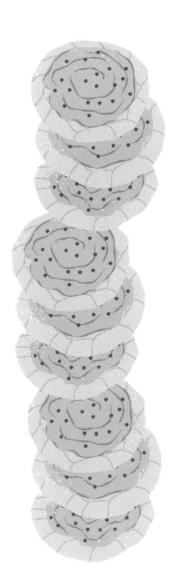

Sugar cookies can be formed by hand or rolled out and cut into shapes, and they are often decorated with frosting and sprinkles during holidays such as Halloween or Christmas. The modern sugar cookie originated in Nazareth, Pennsylvania, when German Protestant settlers created a round, buttery cookie in the mid-1700s, naming it the Nazareth sugar cookie after their hometown. Since then, sugar cookies have taken many forms and become wildly popular.

FUN FOOD FACT
In 2001, House Bill 1892 was passed, designating the Nazareth sugar cookie as the official cookie of the Commonwealth of Pennsylvania.

July 10
PIÑA COLADA DAY

The piña colada, which literally means "strained pineapple," was probably first created in Puerto Rico during the 1950s after Cóco López—cream of coconut—became available. However, rumor has it that the pirate Roberto Cofresi first combined white rum, pineapple juice, and coconut to boost the morale of his crew before his death in 1825. The drink gained worldwide fame following the release of singer-songwriter Rupert Holmes's 1979 hit "Escape (The Piña Colada Song)."

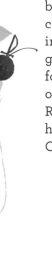

July 11
MOJITO DAY

The oldest-known recipe for a mojito appeared as the "Mojo de Ron" in the Cuban book *Libro de Cocktail*, published in 1929. However, legend has it that the drink was originally offered by natives to the crew of Sir Francis Drake as a remedy for dysentery and scurvy following their 1586 raid of Cartagena, Colombia. Today, the drink is very popular in Britain, and bars in Havana are known to add angostura bitters to balance out the cocktail's sweetness.

July 12
PECAN PIE DAY

The word "pecan" comes from the Algonquin word *pakani*, and indeed there's evidence that these nuts were cultivated by Native Americans of the southern United States thousands of years ago. While the pecan pie's location and date of origin are unknown, this Southern specialty probably arose as a variant of chess pie—one of several tart varieties brought from England to America—in nineteenth-century Texas. More recently, the recipe has been adapted to include ingredients like bourbon whiskey, butterscotch chips, and even chia seeds.

FUN FOOD FACT

The pecan capital of the United States is Albany, Georgia, which has over 600,000 pecan trees and hosts an annual National Pecan Festival.

July 13
FRENCH FRY DAY

If you have ever ordered a hamburger or sandwich anywhere in the world, chances are you were offered a side of French fries. Who hasn't heard of this salty, deep-fried snack? Oddly, it is likely that "French" fries are a Belgian invention of the eighteenth century. In nearly every pub, diner, and fast-food outlet in America, fries are served with ketchup, but in their native Belgium, these pommes frites are usually dipped in mayonnaise.

July 14
GRAND MARNIER DAY

This orange-flavored liqueur was invented by a French wine merchant named Alexandre Marnier-Lapostolle in 1880. Combining sugar and Cognac brandy with the essence of tropical bitter oranges—particularly those of the *Bigaradia* subspecies—Grand Marnier is commonly used in margaritas as well as flambé dishes like crème brûlée and crêpes suzette.

FUN FOOD FACT
Several limited-edition varieties of Grand Marnier have been produced over the years, including Raspberry Peach, which blends European raspberries with rare red peaches from the south of France, and the $220 Sesquicentennial Edition, which was made with fifty-year-old cognacs and sold in special frosted-glass bottles with hand-painted Art Nouveau decoration.

July 15
GUMMY WORM DAY

The perfect Halloween treat, gummy worms were introduced by the candy manufacturer Trolli in the 1980s as a competitor to Haribo's famous gummy bears, which were finally imported to the United States from Germany in 1981. Conceived by German confectioner Hans Riegel in 1922, gummy candy originally contained gum arabic, although today's varieties are gelatin-based. In the 1990s, a furor arose around a possible link between the gelatin contained in gummy candy, which comes from bovine skin and bones, and a mad cow disease outbreak, but the FDA eventually put that concern to rest.

FUN FOOD FACT

In 2005, Kraft Foods, Inc. was forced to stop production of its controversial Trolli Road Kill gummies—partially flattened snakes, squirrels, and chickens—after complaints from animal rights groups.

July 16
CORN FRITTER DAY

The United States produces 40 percent of the world's corn—more than any other country—and it is repurposed in many ways, from corn syrup, to breakfast cereal, to biofuel. For at least a millennium, Native Americans have used ground corn for staple foods like tortillas and arepas, but it wasn't until the Europeans brought their deep-fried cooking techniques to North America that corn fritters emerged in Southern cuisine. Indonesia also has a savory version of the corn fritter known as *bakwan jagung*, which draws comparisons with Japanese tempura.

FUN FOOD FACT

A similar Southern specialty, the hushpuppy, is a deep-fried ball of cornmeal dough, served as a side to seafood and barbecue dishes.

Traditional Corn Fritters

Makes 6 servings

INGREDIENTS

½ cup all-purpose flour

⅓ cup cornmeal

1 tablespoon sugar

1 teaspoon kosher salt

½ teaspoon baking powder

1½ teaspoons chopped fresh
   thyme leaves

½ cup whole milk

3 egg whites

2 cups frozen (thawed) or fresh
   corn kernels

4 tablespoons vegetable oil

1 tablespoon salted butter

DIRECTIONS

1. In a large mixing bowl, sift together the flour, cornmeal, sugar, salt, and baking powder. Stir in the thyme.

2. In a medium mixing bowl, whisk together the milk and egg whites until well combined.

3. Make a well in the middle of the dry ingredients and add the wet ingredients, stirring until combined. It's okay if there are a few lumps.

4. Fold the corn kernels into the batter with a rubber spatula.

5. In a large nonstick skillet over medium heat, heat 2 tablespoons oil and the butter. When the oil is hot, spoon the batter in ¼-cup scoops into the skillet.

6. Cook the fritters for 3 minutes, then flip and cook another 3 minutes on the other side. Transfer to a paper towel–lined plate to drain.

7. Repeat with the remaining batter, adding additional oil as needed.

July 17
PEACH ICE CREAM DAY

It takes twelve pounds of milk to make just one gallon of ice cream. Peaches, a popular addition to ice cream since the early days of the United States, are at peak ripeness during the month of July.

{ *Carrying crates of peaches from the orchard to the shipping shed in Delta County, Colorado, 1940.*

July 18
CAVIAR DAY

True caviar comes from the icy waters of the Caspian Sea, where the environment is most conducive to producing the finest sturgeon, including the world's largest freshwater fish: the beluga sturgeon. Many subspecies of sturgeon are facing extinction, which accounts for caviar's status as a very expensive delicacy. Escargot caviar—salt-cured snail eggs—is an emerging delicacy in countries like Japan, Europe, and the United States. Unlike true caviar, it is whitish in color and has a subtle, earthy "baked asparagus" flavor.

FUN FOOD FACT
Italy is the world's largest exporter of farmed caviar, accounting for 20 percent of the world's caviar consumption.

July 19
DAIQUIRI DAY

Although the daiquiri resembles the British Royal Navy's grog, which was popular in the eighteenth century, the cocktail takes its name from the village and iron mines of Daiquiri near Santiago, Cuba. As one story goes, Jennings Cox, an American mining engineer working there around the year 1900, developed the simple rum-sugar-lime juice recipe to make the local rum more palatable. It later became a favorite of both Ernest Hemingway and John F. Kennedy.

July 20
ICE CREAM SUNDAE DAY

In the decade leading up to the twentieth century, several U.S. cities laid claim to being the birthplace of the ice cream sundae. But the award for the biggest ice cream sundae ever created goes to Anaheim, California, for the twelve-foot-tall sundae built in 1985 with 4,667 gallons of ice cream. Serendipity III in New York City holds the record for most expensive sundae with its thousand-dollar Golden Opulence Sundae covered in 23 karat edible gold leaf.

{ *A soda fountain owner from Southington, Connecticut, making a banana split, 1942.*

July 21
CRÈME BRÛLÉE DAY

The earliest known reference to crème brûlée appears in a French cookbook from 1691, although neighboring Catalonia had an almost identical recipe, known today as *crema catalana*, in the Middle Ages. The world record for largest crème brûlée is held by the Orlando Culinary Academy for its 1,600-pound, 26-foot-wide, 2-million-calorie creation. Nowadays, discs of caramel are often formed directly on top of the custard with a butane torch or by flambéing a hard liquor on it.

July 22
PENUCHE DAY

Penuche, a regional food of New England, might as well be known as vanilla fudge, as it differs from standard fudge in its substitution of brown sugar from white sugar and does not use chocolate, which most fudge recipes use—in New England, maple syrup is also sometimes added. Some food historians think it was invented in 1924, by Mark Penuche, a former Boston Bruins player, but it is not known for certain. The term penuche comes from the Spanish word *panocha*, meaning "raw sugar."

FUN FOOD FACT

In the southern United States, penuche is often called brown sugar fudge candy.

Speedy Crème Brûlée

Makes 6 ramekins

INGREDIENTS

1 quart heavy cream
1 (2-inch) piece vanilla bean, cut in
 half and seeds scraped
2 teaspoons almond extract
1 cup sugar
6 large egg yolks
¼ teaspoon cinnamon
2 quarts hot water

DIRECTIONS

1. Preheat the oven to 325°F. Place 6 ramekins into a large cake pan and set aside.

2. In a medium saucepan, combine the cream, vanilla bean, and seeds. Stir constantly over medium heat until mixture begins to simmer.

3. Remove the saucepan from the heat, stir in the almond extract, cover, and let set for 10 to 15 minutes. Remove the vanilla bean before proceeding.

4. In a medium bowl, whisk together ½ cup sugar, the egg yolks, and the cinnamon until well blended.

5. In a slow and steady stream, while whisking constantly so as to avoid curdling the eggs, add the cream mixture, until well combined.

6. Divide the liquid evenly among the ramekins.

7. Pour the hot water into the pan to surround the ramekins halfway up the sides

8. Carefully transfer the pan to the preheated oven and bake until the crème brûlée is set, 40 to 45 minutes.

9. Remove the ramekins from the pan and refrigerate for at least 2 hours.

10. Equally divide the remaining ½ cup sugar among the 6 dishes and spread on top. Using a torch, melt the sugar to form a caramelized top. Let the crème brûlée sit at least 5 minutes before serving.

July 23
HOT DOG DAY

When someone mentions a hot dog, you might recall idyllic summer baseball games and backyard barbecues. Or maybe the Oscar Mayer Wienermobile comes to mind. Coney Island, home of the notorious hot dog–eating contest, is the birthplace of this all-American food. In 1867 German immigrant Charles Feltman allegedly started serving Frankfurt sausages on long rolls to beachgoers from his pushcart, calling them "Coney Island red hots." After establishing a restaurant, one of his workers went on to found the iconic Nathan's Famous food stand in 1916.

{ *Nathan's Famous hot dog stand on the Coney Island boardwalk, New York City, 1954.*

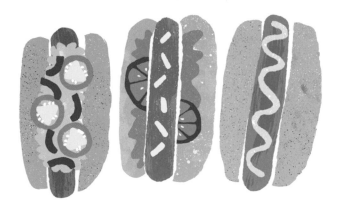

July 24
TEQUILA DAY

This potent spirit has its origin in the Mexican city of Tequila more than five hundred years ago. The blue agave–based drink evolved from *pulque*, a thousand-year-old Mesoamerican alcoholic beverage made from the fermented sap of the agave plant. Mezcal, a similar, smokier Mexican spirit that is rising in popularity, gets its name from the Nahuatl word for "oven-cooked agave," and some bottles are sold *con gueso*—"with worm," or moth larva, to be precise.

July 25
HOT FUDGE SUNDAE DAY

Long disputed are the origins of the first ice cream sundae, and the controversial debate still continues to this day. A couple of cities claim to be the birthplace, including Cleveland, New York, and New Orleans, but the two most contentious rival cities are Two Rivers, Wisconsin, and Ithaca, New York. Two Rivers citizens claim that a soda fountain owner named Ed Berners poured chocolate syrup over a bowl of vanilla ice cream for a customer one day in 1881. It was a hit, and he soon began to serve it every Sunday afterwards. Meanwhile, Ithaca residents argue that one Sunday in 1892, pharmacy owner Chester Platt served a patron, Reverend John Scott, a bowl of vanilla ice cream that he topped with cherry syrup and a candied cherry. Platt named it "Cherry Sunday" in honor of both the day and his reverend patron; however, Platt later changed the name to "sundae" so as not to offend the church.

July 26
BAGELFEST DAY

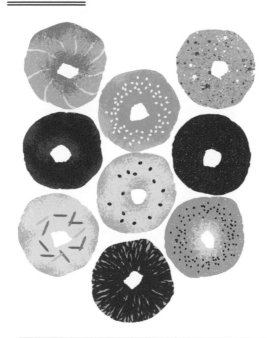

Synonymous with Jewish-American cuisine and New York City, the bagel has a few competing accounts as to its origins; however, it is widely believed Poland's Jewish population is responsible for creating the version of the bagel we know today. The earliest written account is a regulation by the Jewish Council of Krakow, Poland. In fact, many think that the word "bagel" stems from the Yiddish word *beigen*, meaning "to bend." At first, bagels were limited to the upper classes, as only the rich could afford the wheat flour from which they were made, but eventually, like many foods, they became a food for the masses. Bagels arrived with Jewish immigrants to New York City in the late nineteenth century, and were not well known outside of the city and its environs until the 1960s, when Lender's, a family bakery from New Haven, Connecticut, began to sell their frozen bagels nationwide.

July 27

SCOTCH DAY

Scotch refers only to whiskey made in Scotland. It is made mostly from malted barley and has been aged for at least three years in oak barrels. Due to the complex nature of Scotch, many purists prefer their Scotch served "neat," which means a glass with just Scotch and nothing else, or else with a little bit of room-temperature water. The Rob Roy, one of only a handful of mixed drinks featuring Scotch, is made with Scotch, angostura bitters, and sweet vermouth, and topped with a maraschino cherry.

FUN FOOD FACT

Home to several whisky distilleries, Dufftown in northeast Scotland produces more malt whisky than any other Scottish town and has been called the Whisky Capital of the World.

July 28

MILK CHOCOLATE DAY

In 1876, Daniel Peter, a Swiss chocolate maker, decided to devise a chocolate that would differentiate his sweet treats from the creations of rival Swiss chocolatiers. He became inspired by his friend and next-door neighbor Henri Nestlé (the founder of the Nestlé Company), who was using a "milky flour" powder for baby food. After years of experimenting, Peter mixed condensed milk, sugar, and cocoa, and in 1876, created the first milk chocolate formula. He called it "Gala," a root from Greek, meaning, "from the milk."

July 29
LASAGNA DAY

Although lasagna is considered an Italian dish from Naples, there is some evidence that the dish is Greek, from the word *lasanon*, referring to the pot that the dish is cooked in, or *laganon*, the type of pasta. The Romans later changed the name to *lasanum*, which meant "pot." Whether Greek or Roman, the cooking method is similar: sheets of pasta are alternated with layers of fillings (of which there are countless varieties) and then baked.

FUN FOOD FACT

Baked ziti is a similar baked casserole dish that is a staple in Italian-American homes. Instead of layering sheets of pasta, however, this entrée combines ziti macaroni with a cooked cheese and tomato-based sauce that may include sausage, mushroom, and other common foods found in Italian kitchens.

July 30
CHEESE-CAKE DAY

Believe it or not, cheesecakes have been around for a very long time. The ancient Greeks and Romans both made an early form of today's cheesecake with just crushed cheese, wheat flour, and egg. The Romans used the cakes as temple offerings. With the invention of cream cheese in 1872 by William Lawrence, cheesecakes became lighter. There are now countless versions that vary by region and country.

July 31
COTTON CANDY DAY

This sticky, sugary, and colorful treat immediately evokes memories of vacations, amusement parks, and carnivals. Ironically, one of the inventors of the modern cotton candy machine was a dentist, William Morrison, who, along with his partner, introduced it during the 1904 World's Fair and called it Fairy Floss. Later, another dentist, Joseph Lascaux, invented a similar product and called it Cotton Candy in 1921. Known to be notoriously fickle machines, the automated cotton candy machine was invented in 1978 and continues to be used today. Now, the question remains: Just what were those dentists thinking?

FUN FOOD FACT
In Australia, cotton candy is known as "fairy floss."

Food Celebrations This Month

National Catfish Month

National Panini Month

National Peach Month

National Sandwich Month

National Mustard Day (First Saturday of August)

August 1
RASPBERRY CREAM PIE DAY

There are over two hundred different types of raspberries, with the golden variety being the sweetest. Raspberries are used to create new species, such as loganberries, which are a cross between raspberries and blackberries; boysenberries, which are a cross between red raspberries, loganberries, and blackberries; and nessberries, which are a cross between raspberries, blackberries, and dewberries.

FUN FOOD FACT
Raspberries, with their woody, prickly stems, are actually part of the same genus as roses.

August 2
ICE CREAM SANDWICH DAY

The predecessor of the American ice cream sandwich dates to 1899 in New York City, when a pushcart vendor began selling slices of ice cream wedged between two graham wafers for a penny. It was an instant hit, as it allowed customers an easy and neat way to eat ice cream. The modern version we are familiar with was invented in 1963.

August 3
WATERMELON DAY

{ *President Gerald Ford tossing a watermelon in Philadelphia, Pennsylvania, 1976.*

Watermelons are part of the cucurbit family and related to squash, pumpkins, and cucumbers. Japanese farmers grow watermelons inside square boxes, making them fit better inside refrigerators. In Africa and Egypt, watermelons are commonly paired with feta cheese. The feta's salt brings out the watermelon's natural flavor and juice.

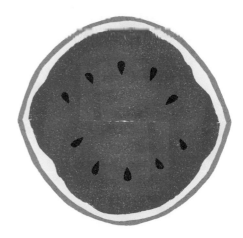

August 4

CHOCOLATE CHIP COOKIE DAY

During the late 1930s, Ruth Wakefield—the inventor of the chocolate chip—also invented her famous Toll House Chocolate Crunch Cookie to serve alongside ice cream at her establishment, the Toll House Inn, in Whitman, Massachusetts. Her recipe first appeared in print in the 1938 edition of Wakefield's *Tried and True Toll House Recipes*. Ruth later sold her Toll House Cookie recipe to Nestlé, which then featured it on their chocolate morsels packaging. Initially, chocolate chip cookies were mostly known on the East Coast, but during World War II, their popularity spread as people on the home front were encouraged to make and send cookies to soldiers. After the war, chocolate chip cookies became one of America's most treasured national desserts.

August 5
OYSTER DAY

There's an old bit of advice that you should not eat fresh oysters during the months without an R in them (i.e., May, June, July, and August) because oysters spawn during the warmer months, which supposedly gives them a weak flavor. Some people, however, disagree with this advice, as today most oysters are farm raised. When the first Dutch settlers arrived to Manhattan, they found a harbor filled with oyster beds. So many oyster beds, in fact, that New York Harbor was supplying half of the world's oysters, and countless oyster houses and taverns thrived in the city until around 1910, when overfishing and water pollution depleted the oyster beds. Thankfully, there has been an effort to rebuild them.

August 6
ROOT BEER FLOAT DAY

{ A soda jerk passing an ice cream soda between two soda fountains, 1936.

While a couple of people claim responsibility for inventing the ice cream float, it is usually Robert McGay Green from Philadelphia, Pennsylvania, who gets full credit. While serving cream sodas to customers at an exhibition in 1874, Green ran out of sweet cream, so he decided to use ice cream instead. Needless to say, his substitution proved to be a huge success, and a malt shop classic was born. Reportedly, he earned $400 in a single day serving his frosty creation. Another version of the story goes that Green, after watching patrons enjoying ice cream and a regular glass of water at a soda shop, came up with the idea of combining ice cream with carbonated water and devised sixteen combinations. Whichever account is true, thank you, Mr. Green, for one deliciously sweet thirst quencher.

August 7
IPA DAY

{ *An Irish American bartender serving beer to British sailors in a bar on Third Avenue in New York City, 1942.*

FUN FOOD FACT
In the United States, IPA's recent surge in popularity is tied to the rise of the hoppy style of craft beer.

Step into any bar, restaurant, or brewery these days, and most likely an array of domestic and foreign IPA beers will be awaiting you. But what exactly is an IPA? An initialism for India Pale Ale, IPAs began to be brewed in England in the late 1700s with extra hop and alcohol, which was needed to prevent the beer from spoiling in long overseas voyages to English colonies. (The term IPA was used in an Australian newspaper in 1829 and it stuck.) A London brewer named George Hodgson is usually credited as the brewmaster behind the IPA. There are three main types: American, English, and Imperial, or Double, with each one having different amounts of malt, hop, and alcohol. Imperial, or Double, IPAs have a lot more hops in addition to a higher alcohol content: above 7.5 percent by volume.

August 8
ZUCCHINI DAY

Zucchini is thought to have been developed in northern Italy from squash that was brought back from the New World by explorers. It then arrived back to the United States around the 1920s with Italian immigrants. *Zucchini* is the plural form of the Italian singular *zucchino*, or "small squash," which stems from *zucca*, meaning "squash. Zucchini blossoms, or *fiori di zucca*, is a popular dish in which the blossoms are battered and then fried, but the most popular zucchini dish is, of course, zucchini bread!

August 9
RICE PUDDING DAY

Spanning many countries and traditions, rice pudding is a dessert staple with a long history. Because it was imported, rice was for hundreds of years considered a luxurious upper-class food. The first English rice pottage recipes, the precursor to puddings, appear in 1390. These savory dishes were meant to mop up meat juices. By the early 1600s, a sweet version with sugar and honey began to be added to the recipes. By the 1700s, rice became a much more common import, making rice an economical food. Nowadays, there are many variations of rice pudding that use coconut milk, cinnamon, ginger, vanilla, rosewater . . . you name it.

Coconut Rice Pudding

Makes 14 servings

INGREDIENTS

½ cup long-grain white rice

1 cup water

1 (13.5-ounce) can coconut milk

1 (14-ounce) can sweetened
  condensed milk

Pinch cinnamon

¼ teaspoon kosher salt

½ cup coconut flakes

1 teaspoon vanilla extract

½ cup sliced toasted almonds,
  for serving

½ cup toasted coconut flakes,
  for serving

DIRECTIONS

1. In a medium saucepan, combine the rice and water over high heat.

2. When the water starts to boil, reduce the heat to low, cover, and simmer for 10 to 12 minutes or until the rice is cooked and the water is absorbed. Fluff the rice with a fork.

3. Pour in the coconut milk, condensed milk, cinnamon, and salt; stir until combined.

4. Place the pan back on low heat and cook for 15 to 20 minutes, or until the rice has thickened and the mixture is creamy.

5. Remove the pan from the heat and mix in the coconut flakes and vanilla.

6. Divide the pudding among 4 serving dishes and refrigerate at least 4 hours before serving.

7. Garnish with the almonds and toasted coconut.

August 10
S'MORES DAY

The first s'mores most likely came from a 1927 recipe called "Some Mores" that was showcased in the guide *Trampling and Trailing with the Girl Scouts*, which included various instructions on building campfires. However, roasting marshmallows was a popular pastime as far back as the 1890s. In 1938, the contraction "s'more" first appeared. As for using chocolate and graham crackers together, the concept had been around for a bit with Mallomar cookies, which were created by Nabisco in 1913 and featured a chocolate-coated confection of marshmallows on top of a graham cracker. MoonPies, which began to be sold in 1917, consisted of graham crackers filled with marshmallow and then dipped in chocolate. Regardless of the inventor, s'mores are a definite "must" for the summer evenings!

August 11
PANINI DAY

Although the first mention of the Italian word *panini* in the United States dates from 1956, the popular lunchtime sandwiches were a product of Milan in the 1970s and 80s, when *paninoteche*, or panini shops, were a trend—so much so that home panini grills began to be sold to the public in 1975. The craze crossed the ocean and hit Manhattan in the 1990s when these tiny sandwiches quickly became the posh new lunch treat. The best thing about paninis is that there are no right or wrong combinations, which means anything goes!

CLASSIC PANINI COMBINATIONS

Asparagus and Goat Cheese

Avocado and Pesto

BLT with Mozzarella and Sundried Tomato

Brie, Turkey, and Spinach

Chicken Caesar

Eggplant and Pesto

Pear, Avocado, Prosciutto, and Arugula

Pear, Brie, and Chicken

Avocado and Mozzarella with Pesto

Prosciutto, Havarti, and Tomato

August 12
JULIENNE FRIES DAY

Like all fancy techniques, julienne (also called *allumette*) is a French method of cutting and slicing, usually vegetables, into thin, long strips, like matchsticks. There are three similar sizes: julienne, which is around ⅛ × ⅛ × 2 inches; batonnet, which is ¼ × ¼ × 3 inches; and baton, which is ½ × ½ × 2½ inches. Julienne fries are also sometimes called shoestring fries.

FUN FOOD FACT
What most people consider the classic French fry size is the batonnet cut.

August 13
FILET MIGNON DAY

Cut from the small end of the tenderloin, filet mignon is the king of luxurious meat cuts. Its name comes from the French *filet*, meaning a "boneless thick cut," and *mignon*, which means "cute or dainty." However, it was American writer William Sydney Porter, known by the pen name O. Henry, who coined the term "filet mignon" in his 1906 book *The Four Million*. Most people prefer their filet mignons on the rarer side, as the cut is extremely tender. Many cooks will also "butterfly" a tenderloin, which means to split it open, so that both sides will cook more evenly.

August 14
CREAMSICLE DAY

Although the term Creamsicle is officially owned by and a registered brand name of Unilever's Good Humor division, the name has become ubiquitous for any popsicle with vanilla ice cream and fruit. The classic Creamsicle is, of course, vanilla ice cream covered with orange sherbet. Its origins are murky, but the invention of popsicles, in general, is credited to Frank Epperson from San Francisco in the early 1920s; he also invented the Fudgsicle and Dreamsicle.

FUN FOOD FACT
In 1905, when he was just eleven years old, Epperson was supposedly successful in encasing vanilla ice cream in a layer of frozen fruit juice.

LEMON MERINGUE PIE DAY

Although meringue has been around since the seventeenth century, our modern lemon meringue pie came about in the nineteenth century, in 1806, when Elizabeth Coane Goodfellow elaborated a lemon custard variation.

{ *Workers hand-grading lemons into trays according to quality in Lamanda Park, California, 1923.*

August 16
RUM DAY

Who would have thought that the Caribbean's prized liquor started as a trash problem? A byproduct from making sugar, molasses was the liquid that resulted from boiling sugar cane and letting it cure to obtain solid sugar. Although molasses was a stellar hit in many recipes up to the twentieth century, sugar cane farmers still had more molasses than they ever needed—they even dumped it into the ocean to get rid of it. Soon it was discovered that molasses could be mixed with the skimmed-off liquid of sugar cane juice and then fermented, turning it into rum. And thus a great liquor was born.

FINE RUM

August 17
VANILLA CUSTARD DAY

There are countless varieties of custards, but the one thing they all have in common is that they employ milk (or cream) and egg yolk. Harking back to the ancient Romans, egg and milk mixtures were popular throughout continental Europe, but it was not until the Middle Ages that sweet custards begin to appear. European settlers brought their custard-making techniques with them to the New World, and in the 1840s, with the invention of custard powder, custard desserts really took off in the United States.

FUN FOOD FACT
Custard is a starting point to a couple of similar fillings, namely pastry cream, or crème pâtissière, when starch is added; confectioners' custard, when sugar or flour is added; crème anglaise, when only egg is used as a thickener; and blancmange, when only starch is used as a thickener and no egg.

August 18
ICE CREAM PIE DAY

{ *A group of women spooning homemade ice cream out of freezers and onto plates with cake, ca. 1935.*

Ice cream in pie form? Sign me up! The origins of this dessert are not known, but many recipes for this creamy treat currently abound. Combine a chocolate wafer crust with vanilla ice cream, caramel sauce, and espresso fudge to create frozen mud pie, or freeze a mixture of crushed pineapple, sweetened condensed milk, and lemon juice on a graham cracker crust for a tropical variation. The possibilities are endless!

August 19
SOFT-SERVE ICE CREAM DAY

{ *An ice cream truck, probably in Washington, D.C., ca. 1918.*

Like many food firsts, soft-serve ice cream has some conflicting origins. J. F. McCullough and his son Alex, the founders of Dairy Queen, or DQ, claim to have invented this summer staple in the mid 1930s after noticing that customers preferred a softer ice cream, served at 23°F, instead of the standard −5°F. After tweaking their ice cream recipe and finding the perfect freezer, they opened the first DQ in 1940. Tom Carvel, the creator of Carvel, also claims to be the first to sell soft serve when his ice cream truck broke down and he quickly sold his melting product as a new dessert. He opened his first Carvel store in 1934.

FUN FOOD FACT

Soft-serve ice cream machines use a liquid mix that is poured into a specialized chamber that churns, freezes, and adds air to it.

August 20
"BACON LOVERS" DAY

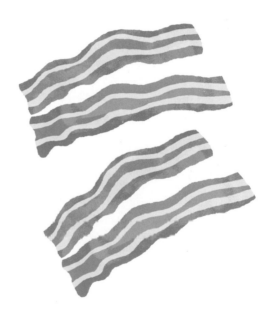

Who doesn't love bacon . . . even vegetarian bacon? Dating back to 1500 B.C. in China, bacon is one of the first processed meats, and Americans are obsessed with it—especially within the last couple of years. From classic dishes like bacon-wrapped scallops to, yes, even bacon ice cream, this pork product is a favorite, with Americans eating almost eighteen pounds a year per person!

FUN FOOD FACT
The expression "bring home the bacon" dates back to twelfth-century England, when married men would receive a portion of bacon from the church if they could swear they did not argue with their wives for a year and a day. Those who did bring home the bacon were considered model citizens in their community.

August 21
SWEET TEA DAY

All you have to do to prepare this ubiquitous Southern libation is brew sugar with black tea and then add ice, but the recipe didn't appear until the 1879 publication of the cookbook *Housekeeping in Old Virginia*. This recipe called for green tea, but following World War II (and the associated antipathy for the Japanese), Americans developed a strong preference for the black tea produced in India.

August 22
"EAT A PEACH" DAY

With the first peach orchard established in Florida in 1565, peaches have long been a Southern specialty. Even though they are considered a Georgian treasure, more than half come from California, with South Carolina in second place, followed by Georgia in third. However, the biggest peach growers in the world are China and Italy.

August 23
CUBAN SANDWICH DAY

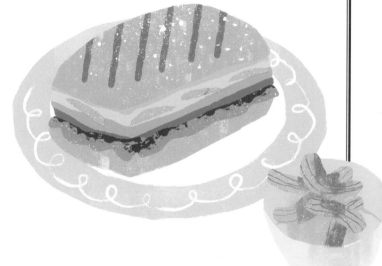

There is fierce debate over which Floridian city, Tampa or Miami, has the best and most authentic Cuban sandwich, or *sandwich cubano*. One's hometown residency has, of course, a slight influence. When the tobacco and cigar industry began in Ybor City in Tampa, Florida, in the late 1880s, many Cuban immigrants settled in the area to work. Soon, the pressed sandwich, made on a grill, or *plancha*, started to appear in local cafés and factory cafeterias. It featured Cuban bread stuffed with layers of ham, pork, Swiss cheese, mustard, pickles, and salami (only in Tampa). Meanwhile in Miami, the sandwich gained popularity with the growing Cuban immigrant community in the 1960s.

FUN FOOD FACT
Because a large Italian community lived alongside the Cubans, the Tampa Cuban sandwich uses salami, while the Miami version does not.

August 24
PEACH PIE DAY

Summer is all about peaches, and celebrating this delicious fuzzy fruit never gets old! There are two types of peaches: Clingstone peaches (harvested from May through August), which have a soft, sweet, and juicy flesh that does not fall off the pit, making them perfect for canning and freezing, and Freestone peaches (harvested late May through October), which have a less juicy, firmer flesh that does fall off the pit, making them ideal for eating fresh.

August 25
WHISKEY SOUR DAY

Appearing in 1862's *The Bartenders Guide* by Jerry Thomas, the whiskey sour has roots that begin with sailors, who would dilute their liquor rations with lime and lemon juice, creating rudimentary early versions of sour cocktails. During Prohibition, sour elements were also added to mask the flavors of bad (aka cheap) liquor, and the whiskey sour had a heyday. During World War II, many distilleries switched their operations to make industrial alcohol for the war effort, and it wasn't until the 1950s and '60s that the whiskey sour came back as a popular drink. Sadly, during the 1980s and '90s, generic sour mixes with sugary and sweet syrups pushed the whiskey sour down on the sophisticated drink scale, but thankfully, due to an increase in artisanal drinks and savvy mixologists, the whiskey sour is now riding its third wave of popularity.

Whiskey Sour

Makes 1 drink

INGREDIENTS

1½ to 2 ounces good whiskey
2 ounces simple syrup
1 ounce lemon juice
Crushed ice
1 Maraschino cherry

DIRECTIONS

1. Stir the whiskey, simple syrup, and lemon juice together. Pour over ice in a tall glass.

2. Add a Maraschino cherry and serve.

{ *A dancer inaugurating the garter flask fad in Washington, D.C., 1926.*

August 26
CHERRY POPSICLE DAY

As the best-selling popsicle flavor, cherry popsicles are the ultimate summertime treat. On June 22, 2005, Snapple attempted to beat the Guinness World Record for the tallest ice pop with a twenty-five-foot-high popsicle in New York City. Unfortunately, they did not achieve their goal, as the frozen kiwi-strawberry mixture melted on the truck from Edison, New Jersey, on its way to the city.

August 27
POTS DE CRÈME DAY

This decadent French dessert dates from the seventeenth century and is made of eggs, egg yolks, cream, milk, vanilla, and chocolate. These little desserts pack a lot of flavor in one little pot!

Pots de Crème

Makes 8 ramekins

INGREDIENTS

2 cups heavy cream, at room
    temperature
5 ounces bittersweet chocolate,
    chopped
½ cup sugar
4 large egg yolks
1 tablespoon coffee-flavored liqueur
    (such as Kahlúa)
1 teaspoon cinnamon
1 teaspoon vanilla extract
¼ teaspoon salt
Whipped cream, for garnish

DIRECTIONS

1. Preheat the oven to 300°F. Place eight 4-ounce ramekins in a shallow baking dish.

2. In a medium saucepan over medium heat, add the cream and heat until it begins to simmer, 5 to 7 minutes.

3. Remove the pan from the heat, and add the chocolate. Stir until the chocolate has melted and mixture is smooth.

4. In a large bowl, whisk together the sugar, egg yolks, liqueur, cinnamon, vanilla, and salt, beating until thickened and lighter in color.

5. Slowly whisk about one-third of the chocolate mixture into the egg mixture. Add the remaining chocolate mixture while stirring constantly until well combined and smooth.

6. Pour the mixture through a fine-mesh sieve and divide the mixture evenly among the ramekins.

7. Transfer the pan with ramekins to the preheated oven and pour enough hot water into the baking pan to reach 1 inch up the outsides of the ramekins.

8. Bake 25 to 30 minutes or until the centers are almost set.

9. Carefully remove the ramekins from the pan and place on a cooling rack to cool for 1 hour.

10. Cover with plastic wrap and chill for at least 1 hour and up to 2 days. Serve chilled or at room temperature, garnished with whipped cream.

August 28
CHERRY TRUNOVERS DAY

Both sweet and savory, turnovers take a filling and then envelop it in folded layers of dough. The term for these portable pies first appeared in 1798 in *Sporting Magazine*.

{ *The Queen of Michigan's National Cherry Festival giving a final once-over and adding finishing touches to a thirty-pound cherry pie to be presented to President Roosevelt at the White House in Washington, D.C., 1939.*

August 29
CHOP SUEY DAY

A Chinese-American dish invented in the United States, chop suey is believed to be inspired by Chinese immigrants, to whom *tsap seui* meant "leftover food" in Cantonese. However, there are many claims of this famous dish's origins, with some scholars positing the dish originated with Chinese railroad workers. Others credit Chinese miners in San Francisco, California, in the 1840s. By the 1950s, there were many prepackaged versions of chop suey; however, as Americans became savvier with their culinary skills and more knowledgeable about food history, traditional Chinese dishes pushed chop suey to the side.

August 30
TOASTED MARSHMALLOW DAY

The word "marshmallow" comes both from the name of its source, the mallow plant, and where it grows, in marshes. The ancient Egyptians are believed to have made the first marshmallows, which were considered sacred and eaten only by royalty to soothe sore throats and heal wounds. They made marshmallows by boiling the root pulp of the mallow plant with sugar until it was thick and then let it cool before straining. By the mid-nineteenth century, the French tweaked the ancient recipe by whipping dried marshmallow root with sugar, egg white, and water and using them as lozenges. By the late 1800s, candy confectioners began to replace the mallow root with gelatin, making a stable marshmallow. Soon after, Americans were introduced to marshmallows and fell in love.

August 31
TRAIL MIX DAY

Combining chocolate, raisins, nuts, and dates, trail mix dates back to 1910 when it was recommended by outdoorsman Horace Kephart as the perfect camping food. Trail mix is also called GORP by many hikers, which is an initialism for "good old raisins and peanuts." Not camping anytime soon? Not a problem. Trail mix can be added to countess dishes such ice cream and fruit.

FUN FOOD FACT
In some Central and Eastern European countries, trail mix is called "student food."

SepTemBeR

Food Celebrations This Month

National Chicken Month

National Honey Month

National Mushroom Month

National Papaya Month

National Potato Month

National Rice Month

September 1
GYRO DAY

The gyro, pronounced either *yee-roh*, *gee-roh*, or *jai-roh*, is a delicious Greek-American pita wrap that many food historians believe was invented in the 1970s in New York City. It is very similar to Turkish *döner kebabs* and Middle Eastern *shawarma*, both of which have been around for hundreds of years. Gyros consist of warm pita bread filled with rotisserie lamb, beef, or chicken rolled up with lettuce, tomatoes, and sauce.

FUN FOOD FACT
Mexican tacos al pastor are also composed of meat shaved from a slowly rotating rotisserie—a cooking method brought to the country by Lebanese immigrants.

September 2
"GRITS FOR BREAKFAST" DAY

Today, we celebrate grits! This breakfast food is a coarse-ground corn porridge usually served as a breakfast item, especially in the South. A staple for many Native Americans, grits were one of the first foods adopted by the early American colonists. Grits are usually prepared by adding one part grits to three parts boiling water, and then they are seasoned with either salt or sugar. Grits are also referred to as *sofkey*, a Native-American word, or hominy.

September 3
WELSH RAREBIT (RABBIT) DAY

Believe it or not, there is no rabbit in Welsh rarebit! Rather, the dish is a savory sauce of melted sharp Cheddar cheese served hot over thick slices of toasted bread. Considered quintessential English pub food, its origins are—as the name suggests—Welsh. Some variations include dark ale, mustard, cayenne pepper, or Worcestershire in the sauce.

FUN FOOD FACT

The unique use of the word rarebit for "rabbit" dates to 1785, and only occurs in reference to this dish, yet the first recorded mention of the dish is from 1725 as rabbit.

September 4

MACADAMIA NUT DAY

Named after John Macadam, a Scottish-born chemist who promoted the nut's cultivation, the macadamia nut is one of Australia's few contributions to the world's food plants. Rich and buttery, it is considered to be one of the most delicious nuts. Since the 1920s, the majority of the world's macadamia nuts are grown on the island of Hawaii, where it was introduced in 1881.

FUN FOOD FACT
Instead of being picked from trees, macadamia nuts are left to ripen and fall before being harvested.

September 5

CHEESE PIZZA DAY

Hailing from Naples, Italy, pizza was originally a poor person's food that was meant to be eaten quickly by the working class who filled the city's waterfront. The first pizzas were sold by street vendors—like many acclaimed dishes—and used various toppings. Flatbreads were not new inventions though; in fact, the ancient Greeks, Romans, and Egyptians were eating them for centuries. When Italian immigrants, many of whom were from southern Italy, came to the United States in search of work, they brought their pizza cravings (and pizza-making skills!) with them. Although the title for first pizzeria in America is hotly contested, Gennaro Lombardi's in Little Italy, New York City, claims to be the first. It opened in 1905. After World War II, Italian-Americans began to migrate to other cities in the States and once again brought their favorite dish with them . . . thankfully!

Cheese Pizza

Makes 8 servings

INGREDIENTS

1½ cups biscuit mix
⅓ cup hot water
1 (8-ounce) can pizza sauce
1 cup shredded sharp Cheddar cheese
1 cup shredded mozzarella cheese
1 teaspoon garlic powder
1 teaspoon Italian seasoning

DIRECTIONS

1. Preheat the oven to 400°F. Grease a 12-inch pizza pan.

2. In a large bowl, stir together the biscuit mix and hot water until a dough forms.

3. Press the dough into the prepared pan and spread the sauce over the dough.

4. Top with the Cheddar, mozzarella, garlic powder, and Italian seasoning.

5. Transfer the pan to the preheated oven and bake until the crust is golden brown and the cheese is bubbly, about 15 minutes.

FUN FOOD FACT

Americans eat approximately one hundred acres of pizza a day.

September 6
COFFEE ICE CREAM DAY

A perfect way to celebrate two delightful foods at once, coffee ice cream was first served in Italian restaurants and cafés as a variation of coffee gelato, a richer variation of ice cream. It is no wonder it is so popular, since every year over four hundred billion cups of coffee are consumed worldwide, making it one of the world's most popular beverages.

FUN FOOD FACT

One scoop of coffee ice cream contains around 100 milligrams of caffeine, the equivalent of a cup of coffee.

September 7
BEER LOVER'S DAY

Cheers! Are you a cerevisaphile—the proper term for a beer lover or enthusiast? Or perhaps you are cenosillicaphobic—fearful of an empty glass. In one variation or another and over all the continents in the world, beer was first served from barrels and then commercially introduced in glass bottles. That all changed in 1962, when Iron City beer became the first to test aluminum cans with a tab opening. By 1970, over 90 percent of all beer was served in a can.

FUN FOOD FACT
English pub patrons used to use mugs with a whistle on the rim to summon servers, hence the origin of "wet your whistle."

September 8
DATE-NUT BREAD DAY

A wholesome alternative to boring, old white bread, date-nut bread uses wheat flour, dates, and nuts. Many recipes add a cup of coffee to give it an even richer flavor. In New England, date-nut bread is often used to make sandwiches or is served toasted with cream cheese.

FUN FOOD FACT
The word "date" comes from the Greek word daktylos, *which means "finger."*

September 9
"I LOVE FOOD" DAY

Today is our day to celebrate everything about food—regardless of whether it is healthy or not! At the very least, it is a good excuse for a cheat day. This food holiday is for those people who spend their lives restricting themselves from what they really would like to be eating. Diets be gone! After all, this is what food holidays are all about, an excuse to eat what you love or try a new food.

September 10

HOT DOG TOPPINGS DAY

The name "hot dog" is credited to sports cartoonist Tad Dorgan, who coined the term during a baseball game in New York in 1901 while watching vendors sell "hot dachshund sausages." He wasn't sure how to spell the word "dachshund," so he shortened it to "hot dog" in his cartoon, but unfortunately, the cartoon cannot be found to prove the story. The term "hot dog" became a popular catchphrase for spectators who would yell to passing food salesmen in the stands. Try these famous hot dog toppings:

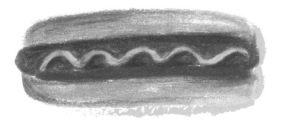

NEW YORK
Boiled dog topped with spicy brown mustard, sauerkraut or sautéed onions, and chili powder.

CHICAGO
Grilled dog topped with fresh tomato, pickle spears, picked hot peppers, chopped sweet onion, and green relish.

DETROIT'S "CONEY DOG"
Boiled dog covered with beef chili, shredded Cheddar cheese, and chopped raw onion.

KANSAS CITY
Grilled all-beef dog topped with melted cheese, sauerkraut, and Thousand Island dressing.

SAN FRANCISCO
Beef dog wrapped in smoked bacon and topped with mayo, pickles, shallots, tomatoes, and shredded lettuce.

September 11

HOT CROSS BUN DAY

A hot cross bun is a spiced sweet bun made with currants or raisins and decorated with icing in the shape of a cross on the top. Most people associate hot cross buns with Good Friday, when they are traditionally eaten, with the cross symbolizing the Crucifixion. Ancient Greeks marked cakes called "soul cakes" with a cross to remember those who had passed. Later, the Saxons honored the goddess Eostre with cakes with a cross on top; it was thought to symbolize the four quarters of the moon. For the first anniversary of 9/11, New York bakers began to sell hot cross buns, or "soul cakes," as a way of remembering those who perished in the attacks.

FUN FOOD FACT

The first recorded reference to "hot cross buns" appeared in a rhyme from the satirical Poor Robin's Almanac *in the early eighteenth century.*

September 12
CHOCOLATE MILKSHAKE DAY

C redit goes to Walgreens's soda jerk Ivar Coulson for making the first milkshake in 1922. By the 1930s, milkshakes were all the rage, especially after Steven Poplawski invented the first electric blender specifically for making shakes. It is probably no surprise that chocolate is one of the most popular flavors.

FUN FOOD FACT

Some say that pressing your tongue against the roof of your mouth or tilting your head back for about ten seconds will stop a "brain freeze" from cold drinks.

September 13
PEANUT DAY

From peanut butter to peanut brittle, we Americans love our peanuts, and there are countless recipes and dishes where this versatile nut is the star ingredient. Four types of peanuts are grown in the United States. The most common is Runner, which is used mostly for peanut butter. Virginia is a large kernel used for snack peanuts and shell peanut products. Spanish has smaller, rounder kernels and is also used for snack peanuts, peanut butter, and confections. And finally, Valencia has a longer pod with three to five kernels in each shell and is used for roasting and boiling.

FUN FOOD FACT

Peanuts are the number-one snack nut consumed in the United States.

September 14
CREAM-FILLED DOUGHNUT DAY

In 1920, Adolf Levitt, a Jewish refugee from Russia, invented the first mechanical doughnut machine, which was able to produce eighty donuts an hour. After World War I, when volunteer "doughnut girls" served American troops doughnuts, this sweet treat really took off. Nowadays, doughnuts can be found in any town and city and are one of Americans' favorite snacks, with countless varieties available. Today, we celebrate cream-filled doughnuts. The sweet dough and creamy filling tempt even the most disciplined. Vanilla and chocolate are tied for most popular filling. The popular Boston cream doughnut features a basic doughnut filled with custard and topped with chocolate frosting, similar to a Boston cream pie but bite size!

FUN FOOD FACT

The Boston cream doughnut was designated the official doughnut of Massachusetts in 2003.

September 15
LINGUINI DAY

Originating in Genoa, Italy, linguini (*linguine* in Italian) means "little tongue." Whether a simple linguini dish with butter and sage or a delicious clam and linguini—which can be served either with a tomato- or white wine–based sauce—there are many ways to enjoy this versatile pasta!

FUN FOOD FACT
A thinner version of linguine, known as linguetinne, *is also available.*

September 16
CINNAMON-RAISIN BREAD DAY

Cinnamon-raisin bread is the original wonder bread. Who would have thought that author Henry David Thoreau would have been the one to invent this sweet bread? (Well, at least according to legend, anyway.) Recipes for raisin bread have existed since 1671, but as far back as the fifteenth century, bread recipes that included raisins were common. Later, during the nineteenth century, raisin bread became a popular snack for high tea in England. Here, in the United States, raisin bread was considered "the bread of iron" during the 1920s, due to the high iron content of raisins.

September 17
APPLE DUMPLING DAY

An apple dumpling is essentially apples, cinnamon, and raisin stuffed inside a pastry. What more could anyone ask for? Apple dumplings are a popular snack among the Pennsylvania Dutch and Amish, as they keep for long periods and can be eaten warm or at room temperature. Although the Pennsylvania Dutch usually eat these fall-flavor treats for breakfast, who says they cannot be eaten at any time? Don't worry, no one will know!

FUN FOOD FACT

The first apple orchard in North America was planted in Boston by Reverend William Blaxton in 1625.

September 18
CHEESEBURGER DAY

{ *A concessionaire making a hamburger at the State Fair in Donaldsonville, Louisiana, 1938.*

What could be more American than cheeseburgers or hamburgers? The history behind America's iconic dish starts in Hamburg, Germany, which was known for its high-quality meats and butchers. As German immigrants arrived in the United States in the mid-nineteenth century, they brought "Hamburg-style" chopped steak. In 1867, New York doctor James H. Salisbury began to promote his "Salisbury Steak" patties as a cure for digestive ailments. At the 1904 World's Fair in St. Louis, Americans were introduced to today's hamburgers. Cheese was added during the late 1920s when Lionel Sternberger decided, in 1926, to add a slice of American cheese to a burger while working as fry cook at the Rite Spot restaurant in Pasadena, California.

FUN FOOD FACT
More than forty billion hamburgers are served in the United States each year.

Homemade Hamburgers

Makes 4 hamburgers

INGREDIENTS

1 pound ground beef
½ cup packed light brown sugar
1 tablespoon steak sauce
1 teaspoon creole seasoning
1 teaspoon garlic powder
4 hamburger buns
Dijon mustard

DIRECTIONS

1. In a large bowl, mix the ground beef with the brown sugar, steak sauce, creole seasoning, and garlic powder. Shape into 4 large patties.

2. Grill the patties over medium heat, 3 to 6 minutes per side, or until desired doneness: closer to 3 minutes for medium-rare and closer to 6 minutes for well-done burgers.

3. Serve the burgers on toasted buns topped with a generous amount of Dijon mustard.

September 19
BUTTER- SCOTCH PUDDING DAY

There is nothing more satisfying than the buttery vanilla taste of butterscotch pudding, but what exactly is "butterscotch"? Butterscotch is a confectionary that contains brown sugar and butter. Although similar to toffee, butterscotch differs in that it is boiled to the soft crack stage and not the hard crack stage like toffee. When it is mixed with cream, it becomes a delicious sauce for topping ice cream, or it can be made into butterscotch pudding, today's celebratory food.

September 20
RUM PUNCH DAY

Cheers! Time to celebrate one of the oldest mixed drinks around. The word "punch" is derived from a Sanskrit word, *pañc*, meaning "five," since the drink was first made with five ingredients: alcohol, sugar, lemons, water, and tea. English sailors in the 1650s brought the recipe for this tasty concoction from India to England. The early colonists were huge fans of rum, and soon added their favorite spirit to their punches in the late 1690s, when Jamaican rum became available.

FUN FOOD FACT
Southern bourbon punch is a popular drink, especially during the annual Kentucky Derby, involving sweet tea, citrus, and—of course— Kentucky bourbon whiskey.

Coconut Rum Punch

Makes 8 to 12 servings

INGREDIENTS

1 cup coconut rum
2 cups orange juice
2 cups pineapple juice
2 cups ginger ale
1 cup grenadine
Orange slices and Maraschino
    cherries, for garnish

DIRECTIONS

1. In a punch bowl, mix together the rum, juices, ginger ale, and grenadine.

2. Serve over crushed ice and garnish with an orange slice and cherry.

September 21
PECAN COOKIE DAY

Pecan cookies are usually small cookies with half-pecan pieces baked into the center. In the South, pecan cookies were often the perfect food to make and give as a gift, since pecans historically have symbolized peace and prosperity. The word *pecan* comes from the Algonquian language and means "stone," and the term was applied to any nut that contains one, such as walnuts and hickory nuts.

FUN FOOD FACT

Commercial growing of pecans did not begin until the 1880s in the United States.

September 22
ICE CREAM CONE DAY

Many believe that the ice cream cone, whether a sugar cone or a waffle cone, is the best way to eat a scoop. The first ice cream cone was made in 1896 by Italo Marchiony in New York City. However, even though Marchiony is credited as the inventor, Ernest A. Hamwi, a Syrian concession-stand owner, sold his waffle-like cookies, called *zalabias*, during the 1904 World's Fair in St. Louis next to an ice cream vendor. When ice cream dishes ran out, Hamwi decided to wrap the ice cream inside one of his zalabias like a cone. It was quickly dubbed a "cornucopia," and the rest is ice cream history.

September 23

WHITE CHOCOLATE DAY

Chocolate lovers, brace yourselves. White chocolate is not actually chocolate. When chocolate is made, cocoa beans are fermented, dried, roasted, and cracked open. The insides, called cacao nibs, are ground into a paste called chocolate liquor. The liquor is separated into two parts: cocoa butter and cocoa solids. The solids give chocolate both the flavor and color that we associate with dark chocolate; however, white chocolate contains only cocoa butter. Milk, sugar, and vanilla are added to make white chocolate.

FUN FOOD FACT
According to the FDA, to be labelled as white chocolate, the product must contain 20 percent cocoa butter, 14 percent milk solids, and 3.5 percent milk fat.

September 24

CHERRIES JUBILEE DAY

Cherries jubilee is a dessert made with cherries, white cake, fruit sauce, and a strong liqueur, usually Kirshwasser, a cherry-flavored brandy. It is then flambéed and served over vanilla ice cream. The original recipe is credited to Auguste Escoffier, who prepared the dish for Queen Victoria's Jubilee in 1897.

September 25

FOOD SERVICE WORKERS DAY

Today we celebrate all of the women and men who dedicate their time and patience to the food service industry. It is to them that we owe our deepest gratitude for making our food experiences not only tasty but also joyous occasions! Thank you!

{ *A waiter at the Sixty-Eight Restaurant in New York City, 1943.*

September 26

KEY LIME PIE DAY

A slice of tart lime custard pie served in a graham cracker crust tastes as smooth as a summer's breeze. Local lore has it that the first Key lime pie was created by an anonymous woman named Aunt Sally, who was the home cook of Key West millionaire William "Bill" Curry. Curry brought condensed milk (invented in 1856 by Gail Borden) to the Keys in the late 1850s. Fresh milk and ice were not available to residents of the Florida Keys until the 1930s when the Overseas Highway was built. Prior, cooks had to rely on sweetened condensed milk, which is a key ingredient in Key lime pie—other than the Key limes, of course. The first printed recipes for this delicious citrus dessert began to appear in the 1930s.

FUN FOOD FACT
True Key limes are very difficult to find, as most were destroyed by a hurricane in 1926. Persian limes were planted in their place.

Key Lime Pie

Makes 8 servings

INGREDIENTS

2 limes, zested
3 large egg yolks
1 (14-ounce) can sweetened
    condensed milk
⅔ cup Key lime juice
1 prepared graham cracker piecrust
Whipped cream, for garnish

DIRECTIONS

1. Preheat the oven 350°F. In a medium bowl with a handheld mixer on medium speed, mix together the lime zest and egg yolks until light and creamy, about 3 minutes. Add the condensed milk and lime juice and beat for another 3 to 4 minutes.

2. Pour the mixture into the prepared piecrust. Transfer the pie to the oven, and bake for 10 to 12 minutes.

3. Turn the oven off and leave the pie inside for 20 more minutes.

4. Transfer the pie to a wire rack to cool, and then place it in the refrigerator to chill for at least 1 hour. Serve with whipped cream.

September 27

CHOCOLATE MILK DAY

Sir Hans Sloane, an Irish botanist, is usually credited with being the "inventor" of chocolate milk after spending time in Jamaica in the early 1700s. While there, he tried a local drink that used cocoa. After finding the drink to be nauseating, he added cocoa to milk and introduced it to England upon his return. It was soon considered a "medicinal" cure. However, Jamaicans were brewing fresh cacao shavings with milk and cinnamon for a long time before Sir Hans arrived.

September 28

STRAWBERRY CREAM PIE DAY

For generations, cooks have combined whipped cream and fresh strawberries. Some recipes call for a custard or pudding base while others use a cream cheese or whipped cream base. Any which way one chooses is perfectly fine. Can anything taste bad with strawberries in it?

Strawberry Cream Pie

Makes 8 servings

INGREDIENTS

2 (8-ounce) packages cream cheese, softened to room temperature
⅔ cup sugar
1 teaspoon vanilla extract
2 cups heavy cream
1 prepared graham cracker piecrust
2 cups strawberries, sliced

DIRECTIONS

1. In a large bowl with a handheld mixer, combine the cream cheese, sugar, and vanilla, and mix until completely combined, about 2 minutes.

2. In a separate large bowl, beat the heavy cream on high speed until peaks form.

3. Fold the whipped cream into the cream cheese mixture, mixing until just combined.

4. Spoon the mixture into the piecrust, and spread it evenly with a spatula.

5. Arrange the strawberry slices in rows around the top of the pie.

6. Chill for at least 2 hours until set.

FUN FOOD FACT

Today's garden strawberry was first bred in Brittany, France, in the 1750s.

September 29
COFFEE DAY

Although coffee had been popular in Europe since the early seventeenth century, it did not gain popularity in the United States until the early eighteenth century. Before the Boston Tea Party in 1773, the early colonists preferred tea as their hot drink of choice. Afterwards, it became more patriotic to start drinking coffee. By the 1860s, coffee had really caught on when James Folger founded the J. A. Folger Coffee Company in San Francisco, and Jabez Burns from New York was granted a patent for the first coffee roaster that did not need to be next to a fire. In 1886, Joel Cheek began to sell a select blend of coffee named Maxwell House after the fancy Maxwell House Hotel in Nashville, Tennessee, which served it. During the Prohibition era in the 1920s, coffee sales took off and we have been coffee aficionados ever since.

FUN FOOD FACT

President Theodore Roosevelt is said to have created Maxwell House's famous brand slogan "Good to the Last Drop" after finishing a cup at the Maxwell House Hotel in 1907.

September 30

MULLED CIDER DAY

For centuries, mulled cider was a common drink throughout Europe and colonial America, where cider apples are commonly found. Cider apples are different from other varieties in that they contain tannin. "Mulling" means heating a beverage slowly with spices, and the most common ingredients in this festive drink are cloves, nutmeg, cinnamon, and allspice. Although mulled cider dates to the ancient Romans, it continues to be popular in England, where it used to be called *wassail*. It is still mentioned in different Christmas carols as "wassailing," which meant happy times and good wishes for a successful apple harvest for the next year.

FUN FOOD FACT

Rosé apple cider is created using red "applecrabs"—hybrids of apples and crabapples.

OctoBER

Food Celebrations This Month

National Apple Month

National Applejack Month

National Caramel Month

National Cookbook Month

National Cookie Month

National Dessert Month

National Pasta Month

National Pickled Peppers Month

National Pizza Month

National Popcorn Poppin' Month

National Pork Month

National Pretzel Month

October 1
PUMPKIN SPICE DAY

Pumpkin spice has been quite a trendy flavor these days and can be found in practically everything, including coffee, milk, ice cream, chewing gum, yogurt, and even steak sauce! But move past the bottled pumpkin spice in the supermarket, as the blend can easily be made at home with cinnamon, nutmeg, ginger, cloves, and allspice.

FUN FOOD FACT
The Pumpkin Spice Latte is Starbucks's most popular seasonal beverage.

October 2
WORLD FARM ANIMALS DAY

Today we celebrate all of the world's farm animals, from sheep, cattle, goats, pigs, and horses to chickens, buffalo, cows, dogs, and cats. Life would be very dull without these beautiful creatures, and each one deserves a collective hug of appreciation.

FUN FOOD FACT
Sheep have excellent memories and can remember as many as fifty acres for up to two years!

October 3
SOFT TACO DAY

Composed of a corn or wheat tortilla folded over a meat filling, soft tacos are as popular as ever. Each region in Mexico specializes in countless varieties, with some using fish as the star ingredient while others use *carnitas*, or pork, and *carne asada*, or sliced, roasted meat.

FUN FOOD FACT

Tacos al pastor *were first called* tacos arabes, *or Arab tacos, because Lebanese immigrants who arrived in Mexico added lamb to tacos. The recipe changed over the years to use pork instead of lamb and to add pineapple.*

October 4
TACO DAY

We Americans love our tacos—so much so that there are two taco celebrations this month. One of the first mentions of tacos in the United States dates to a 1905 San Antonio newspaper article—at that time many Mexicans came to the States to work in mines and railroads. By the 1940s, Mexican cookbooks were giving instructions on how to make hard shell tacos. Fast forward to today, where there has been a reemergence of fast-food trucks, and, not surprisingly, tacos are a popular item, with various culinary traditions, such as Vietnamese, Korean, and Thai, also adopting the taco to showcase their ingredients.

{ *Preparing tortillas in Aguas Calientes, Mexico, ca. 1880–97.*

FUN FOOD FACT

One of the first taco trucks is believed to have been started in New York City by two housewives in 1966.

Chicken Tacos

Makes 6 tacos

INGREDIENTS

2 teaspoons cumin

2 teaspoons chipotle chili powder

½ teaspoon cayenne powder

1 teaspoon kosher salt

½ teaspoon freshly ground black pepper

¼ cup olive oil

1 cup diced white onion

3 garlic cloves, minced

1 pound boneless, skinless chicken thighs, sliced

12 medium corn tortillas

2 avocados, diced

2 jalapeños, diced

3 tablespoons chopped fresh cilantro

1 lime, cut into wedges

DIRECTIONS

1. Preheat the oven to 400°F. Line a baking sheet with foil and set aside.

2. In a small bowl, combine the cumin, chipotle chili powder, cayenne, salt, and pepper.

3. Mix the spices with the oil, ¼ cup onions, and garlic.

4. In a medium bowl, mix together the chicken and spice mixture.

6. Lay chicken in a single layer on the prepared baking sheet.

7. Transfer the baking sheet to the oven and bake for 18 to 22 minutes or until cooked through.

8. Remove the chicken from oven, and when cool enough to handle, shred into bite-sized pieces.

9. Warm tortillas in a hot skillet for a few seconds on each side.

10. To serve, stack two tortillas together and fill each with the chicken, remaining onions, avocado, jalapeños, cilantro, and a squeeze of lime. Serve immediately.

October 5
APPLE BETTY DAY

A favorite dessert of President Ronald Regan, apple betty is a kind of brown betty, a dessert of fruit baked between layers of buttered crumbs. Betties were popular with the early colonists, as the ingredients were easy to find. One of the first betty recipes appeared in 1864 in the *Yale Literary Magazine*.

October 6
NOODLE DAY

Whether Italian, Indonesian, Japanese, Chinese, Thai, or Filipino, noodles are one of the best human inventions and are more popular than ever. There's evidence that noodles have been made from flour and water since 2000 B.C. in China. Noodles are low in fat and have a very low sodium content, so never feel guilty eating them!

Chicken Noodle Casserole

Makes 8 servings

INGREDIENTS

Nonstick cooking spray
2 cups diced cooked chicken breast
2 (10-ounce) cans cream of chicken
  soup
½ cup mayonnaise
½ cup sour cream
½ cup diced onion
1 cup shredded mozzarella cheese
1 cup shredded Cheddar cheese
1½ cups frozen peas and carrots
1 (12-ounce) bag egg noodles, cooked
  according to package directions
  and drained
1 cup Italian breadcrumbs
½ cup (1 stick) salted butter, melted

DIRECTIONS

1. Preheat the oven to 350°F. Spray a 9 x 13-inch baking dish with nonstick cooking spray.

2. In a large bowl, combine the chicken, soup, mayonnaise, sour cream, onion, cheeses, and frozen peas and carrots. Stir until well combined.

3. Stir in the cooked egg noodles and pour the mixture into the prepared baking dish. Top with the breadcrumbs and pour the melted butter evenly over the top.

4. Transfer the dish to the preheated oven and bake for 30 to 35 minutes, or until the top is golden brown.

FUN FOOD FACT
The first noodles eaten in outer space were instant ramen noodles.

October 7
FRAPPÉ DAY

When people say "frappé," many think of a modern take on an old slushy-like coffee drink called "café frappe à la glace" that was popular in the early nineteenth century, but in fact "frappé" has many meanings, depending on where one is from. In New England, frappés are the equivalent of what other states call "milkshakes," and use ice cream, milk, and flavoring. A milkshake, on the other hand, is simply milk and flavoring that is blended or shaken until frothy, while a cabinet is another name for a frappé in certain parts of Rhode Island and southern Massachusetts (cabinet referring to the place that blenders are usually stored). The word "frappé" is also used to describe a Greek instant-coffee drink created in 1957. And, to confuse frappé consumers further, there are also many frappé variations at many national coffee chains. Regardless of where or what kind of frappé you are drinking, enjoy it today!

October 8
FLUFFER-NUTTER DAY

A Fluffernutter is a sandwich made with peanut butter and marshmallow fluff—a combination of melted marshmallows and corn syrup—usually served on white bread. In 1913, Amory and Emma Curtis created their version, called the Snowflake Marshmallow Creme. Emma later published a peanut-butter-and-marshmallow-cream sandwich recipe titled the "Liberty Sandwich" in a promotional booklet in 1918. Meanwhile, Archibald Query began selling his version of marshmallow spread in Somerville, Massachusetts, in 1917. Query later sold his recipe to H. Allen Durkee and Fred Mower, who sold and marketed it as Marshmallow Fluff. By the 1960s, the Fluffernutter sandwich was a common dish in American homes.

FUN FOOD FACT
The "Elvis-style" Fluffernutter sandwich uses bananas, peanut butter, and marshmallow fluff.

October 9
PIZZA & BEER DAY

What could possibly be a better combination than pizza and beer? Whether you're enjoying a Chicago deep-dish pizza (created in 1943 by Pizzeria Uno's founder Ike Sewell, although there is controversy over this claim) or Hawaiian pizza (invented by native Greek Sam Panopoulos in 1962), beer is the perfect complement. Try an IPA (India Pale Ale) or a classic Budweiser, which was created in 1876 by Carl Conrad & Co., in Saint Louis, Missouri. Whatever you choose, sit back and enjoy.

FUN FOOD FACT
Pabst Blue Ribbon beer, established in 1844 by Pabst Brewing Company in Milwaukee, Wisconsin, was once sold with silk ribbons tied around the bottles; however, it quickly became expensive and time-consuming.

October 10
ANGEL FOOD CAKE DAY

Thought to be a spinoff of sponge cake, angel food cake is believed to have originated in the early nineteenth century and received its name due to its lightness. The first white sponge cake recipe appeared in 1839, in Lettice Bryan's cookbook, *The Kentucky Housewife*. In 1878, Isabella Stewart's *The Home Messenger Book of Tested Recipes, Second Edition*, contained a recipe for "Angel's Food Cake." Before Herbert Johnson invented the electric mixer in 1908, beating egg whites was an arduous task that required a lot of arm strength.

October 11
SAUSAGE PIZZA DAY

Sausage is the second most popular pizza topping in the United States. Derived from the Latin word *salsisium*, meaning "salted," sausage comes in many different shapes (loose, crumbled, and patties) and flavors from mild to sweet. Italian-American sausage is usually made with pork and fennel or anise, with hot pepper flakes creating the "hot" variety, but each region in Italy has its own unique version.

{ *Workers making sausage links in Chicago, Illinois, 1927.*

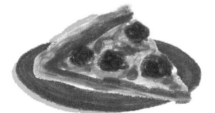

Pepperoni & Sausage Pizza Dip

Makes 10 servings

INGREDIENTS

8 ounces cream cheese, softened to room temperature

2 teaspoons dried Italian seasoning

1 teaspoon garlic powder

2 cups shredded mozzarella cheese

½ cup grated Parmesan cheese

½ cup shredded sharp provolone cheese

1 cup tomato sauce

½ pound cooked loose sausage meat

½ cup mini pepperoni

Toasted bread, for serving

DIRECTIONS

1. Preheat the oven to 350°F. Grease an 8 x 8-inch baking dish with olive oil.

2. In a medium bowl, combine the cream cheese, Italian seasoning, and garlic powder. Spread it in the bottom of the prepared baking dish.

3. Sprinkle half of the cheeses over the cream cheese. Spread the tomato sauce evenly on top. Sprinkle with the sausage and the remaining cheese. Top with the pepperoni.

4. Transfer the dish to the preheated oven and bake for 15 minutes.

5. Serve warm with toasted bread.

October 12
PUMPKIN PIE DAY

FUN FOOD FACT

About 90 to 95 percent of processed pumpkins in the United States are from Illinois.

A classic autumn dish that every American knows well, pumpkin pie is a definite favorite. Native to Central America and cultivated since 5500 B.C., pumpkins and squash were one of the first foods to be brought back to Europe after the New World was discovered. The English were very adept at making pies. By the time the Pilgrims landed on Plymouth Rock, food historians think that they would have been familiar with pumpkin and able to apply their pie-making skills immediately. Early versions of pumpkin pie differed greatly from those of today. Seventeenth-century French cookbooks recommend boiling the pumpkin in milk, draining it, and then adding it to the piecrust. There are a couple of pumpkin pie recipes in Amelia Simmon's 1796 cookbook *American Cookery*, the first known cookbook published in the colonies; one of the recipes is a custard variation similar to today's pumpkin pie.

October 13
YORKSHIRE PUDDING DAY

Yorkshire pudding is a classic English food. It is not a soft pudding in the American sense of the word, but rather a light and puffy savory popover. Made with a batter of milk or water, flour, and eggs, it is placed in baking pans, ramekins, or muffin tins, and used to sop up meat gravies and sauces. The origins of this traditional side dish for the Sunday roast are not known, but the name "Yorkshire" was added to the term "pudding" in the 1747 cookbook *The Art of the Cookery Made Plain and Simple* by Hannah Glasse, as a means of differentiating Glasse's light and crispy pudding from varieties from different regions. In some areas, these puddings were known as "dripping puddings."

October 14
DESSERT DAY

Today, we celebrate everything that is dessert related. No one will pay attention to what you are eating, so pull out your favorite sugar-laden pleasure and go at it!

FUN FOOD FACT
In much of Central and West Africa, there is no tradition of a dessert course following a meal.

October 15
MUSHROOM DAY

Mushrooms have been a part of the human diet for thousands of years. Egyptian pharaohs prized mushrooms as a delicacy, and the ancient Greeks believed that mushrooms gave strength to soldiers in battle. It was the French, however, that began to cultivate fungi in the middle of the seventeenth century, a practice the English later developed. This mushroom cultivating know-how did not reach the United States until the nineteenth century, when in 1891, William Falconer from New York published *Mushrooms: How to Grow Them*, the first-known American book about mushroom growing.

FUN FOOD FACT

The biggest mushroom grower in the world is China, which produces almost 70 percent of the world's mushrooms.

Penne Alla Funghi

Makes 4 servings

INGREDIENTS

1 pound penne or ziti
1 tablespoon olive oil
1½ pounds mixed wild mushrooms, sliced
1 cup white wine
1 cup half-and-half
2 teaspoons chicken bouillon
1 tablespoon flour
¼ teaspoon garlic powder
½ teaspoon crushed red pepper
Kosher salt and freshly ground black pepper
2 cups shredded mozzarella cheese
½ cup grated Parmesan cheese

DIRECTIONS

1. Preheat the oven to 350°F. Grease a 9 x 13-inch baking dish with olive oil.

2. Cook the pasta according to the package directions. Reserve 1 cup of the cooking liquid. Drain and set aside.

3. In a large sauté pan, heat the oil over medium heat. Add the mushrooms and sauté for 5 minutes. Add the wine and let simmer for an additional 2 minutes.

4. In a medium bowl, whisk together the half-and-half, bouillon, flour, garlic powder, and crushed red pepper. Add this mixture to the mushrooms and stir until combined. Cook for another 3 minutes.

5. Add the pasta, along with the pasta cooking liquid, to the mushroom sauce. Turn off the heat and season with salt and pepper to taste.

6. Layer the pasta mixture with mozzarella cheese in the prepared dish in two layers. Sprinkle with the Parmesan.

7. Transfer the dish to the preheated oven and bake for 20 minutes or until golden brown and bubbly.

October 16
NATIONAL LIQUEUR DAY

Although both liqueurs and liquors contain alcohol, there is a difference between the two. A liqueur is a distilled spirit that is sweetened with fruit, herbs, spices, flowers, or fruit, such as peppermint schnapps, Kahlúa, or Cointreau. Liquor is distilled alcohol that is made from fermented grains, such as vodka, gin, brandy, and whiskey. To complicate matters more, liquors can be a base spirit for liqueurs. In the United States, cordial is another term used to refer to liqueurs.

FUN FOOD FACT

The French terms apéritif *and* digestif *can also be confusing. An apéritif (aperitivo in Italian) is meant to stimulate the appetite and to be consumed before a meal; therefore, it is usually low in alcohol and dry, like vermouth and dry sherry. A digestif (digestivo in Italian) is meant to be sipped after a meal to help digestion; common digestifs include port, brandy, and sweet liqueurs.*

October 17
PASTA DAY

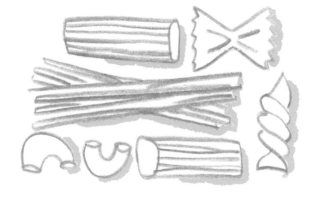

The United States is obsessed with pasta, with the average American consuming twenty pounds of pasta annually. With more than six hundred pasta shapes available around the world, no one can ever say they are sick of pasta! Plus, it is one of the most affordable meals.

FUN FOOD FACT
The Italian term al dente *means "to the tooth" and refers to pasta that has some resistance when you bite into it. Most Italians prefer their pasta al dente, which to them means it is perfectly cooked.*

October 18
CHOCOLATE CUPCAKE DAY

Chocolate and cupcakes, two foods that on their own are perfect, but when combined are sublime and celebrated today!

October 19
SEAFOOD BISQUE DAY

Although today bisques are synonymous with haute cuisine, the origin of these hearty soups is, like many food histories, decidedly working class. The first mention of seafood bisque surfaces in the seventeenth century and references not a luxurious soup but, rather, a simple one with a base of seafood shells, leading historians to conclude it was a practical and frugal attempt to capture the flavor of the seafood. Some claim the word *bisque* comes from the Bay of Biscay in France, but more likely it stems from the French words *bis*, meaning "twice," and *cuites*, meaning "cooked," since the shells are first roasted and then later simmered in a broth. Afterward, a roux or cream is used to thicken it.

Dark Chocolate Cupcakes

Makes 12 cupcakes

INGREDIENTS

Cupcakes

3 ounces dark chocolate, finely
   chopped
⅓ cup cocoa powder
¾ cup hot brewed coffee
¾ cup all-purpose flour
¾ cup granulated sugar
½ teaspoon kosher salt
½ teaspoon baking soda
6 tablespoons vegetable oil
2 large eggs
2 teaspoons white vinegar
1 teaspoon vanilla extract

Frosting

1¼ cups (2½ sticks) unsalted butter,
   at room temperature
1 cup powdered sugar
¾ cup cocoa powder
½ teaspoon salt
¾ cup corn syrup
1 teaspoon vanilla extract
8 ounces dark chocolate, chopped,
   melted, and cooled

DIRECTIONS

1. Preheat the oven to 350°F. Line a 12-cup muffin pan with cupcake liners.

2. To make the cupcakes: In a medium mixing bowl, place the chopped chocolate and cocoa powder. Add the hot coffee and whisk until smooth. Refrigerate for 20 minutes.

3. Meanwhile, in a large bowl, whisk together the flour, granulated sugar, salt, and baking soda; set aside.

4. Remove the chocolate mixture from the refrigerator and whisk in the oil, eggs, vinegar, and vanilla until smooth.

5. Add the flour mixture to the wet ingredients and whisk until smooth.

6. Divide the batter evenly in the muffin pan cups.

7. Transfer the pan to the oven and bake until the cupcakes are set, 17 to 19 minutes.

8. Cool the cupcakes in the pan on a wire rack for 10 minutes.

9. Remove the cupcakes from the pan and transfer them to a wire rack to cool completely before frosting.

10. To make the frosting: In a food processor, blend the butter, powdered sugar, cocoa powder, and salt until smooth.

11. Add the corn syrup and vanilla. Mix until combined, 5 to 10 seconds. Scrape the sides of the bowl, and then add the melted chocolate and pulse until smooth, 10 to 15 one-second pulses.

12. Frost the cupcakes as desired.

October 20
BRANDIED FRUIT DAY

Traditionally, brandy—which is distilled from different fruits like grapes, apples, apricots, blackberries, and wine—pairs well with fruit, and so brandying fruit became a perfect method for preserving summer fruit. Depending on the region of origin and the fruit used, brandy can be divided into several categories: cognac, Armagnac, American brandies, and fruit brandies.

October 21
PUMPKIN CHEESECAKE DAY

Since it is October, we cannot go too many days without celebrating pumpkins, and pumpkin cheesecake is one more example. American colonists were familiar with cheese cakes from the Old World, which used curd cheese and had been popular for centuries. Cream cheese was not developed until 1872, and it gave cheesecakes the richer, lighter, and creamier texture that we know today. As for the flavors, well, anything goes, and today's flavor is pumpkin.

FUN FOOD FACT

Arnold Reuben, a German-Jewish immigrant who owned restaurants in Manhattan, is credited with creating the famous New York cheesecake after experimenting with a cheese pie recipe in 1929. The legendary Lindy's Restaurant, located in Manhattan's Theater District, propelled the New York cheesecake to iconic status.

October 22
NUT DAY

With thousands of different types and varieties, nuts are extremely versatile and can be consumed as a quick snack, featured as a main ingredient, or added as a garnish to a dish. Some nuts have the strangest properties though. Cashews, for example, are in the same plant family as poison ivy and poison sumac, but thankfully the oil that causes itching is contained almost entirely in their shells. Pistachio shells are naturally cream colored, but for a long time were commonly dyed red or green to hide imperfections—nowadays, it is hard to find them due to the decline in the use of food dyes.

October 23
BOSTON CREAM PIE DAY

A Boston cream pie is a cake that is filled with a custard or cream filling and frosted with chocolate icing. Although it is called a Boston cream pie, it is, in fact a cake, and not a pie. It is claimed to have been created in 1856 by Armenian-French chef M. Sanzian at the Parker House Hotel in Boston. He called it Chocolate Cream Pie. The first mention of Boston cream pie appears in the *Methodist Almanac* in 1872.

October 24
BOLOGNA DAY

{ *Two women having lunch at a luncheonette, 1964.*

Bologna, also known as baloney and bolony, is an American classic, which can either bring very happy memories, such as special lunches made at home for a snow day, or unpleasant ones if it was eaten every day in a packaged lunch. American bologna's ancestor is mortadella, which comes from Bologna, Italy, where it is a delicacy made under very strict (and centuries-old) standards. How it came to America is a little murky, but it was associated with German immigrants. It was—and still is—an extremely affordable product that keeps well, and during the Great Depression it served many struggling households. As sandwiches gained in popularity in the 1920s, so did bologna, and it was a staple at many sandwich shops and luncheonettes. Although bologna has fallen out of fashion, there has been a reemergence lately of artisanal bologna.

October 25
GREASY FOODS DAY

There is certainly no shortage of greasy food in the big ol' US of A! There are countless fast-food joints and plenty of diners to fill the need when you have a hankering for onion rings or deep-fried steak. There aren't a lot of foods that don't have a deep-fried version, actually, such as the recent popularity surge of the Deep Fried Oreo.

FUN FOOD FACT
American fast-food restaurants serve an average of 50 million customers every day.

October 26
MINCEMEAT DAY

Mincemeat was originally a medieval mixture of chopped meat (usually beef, venison, or suet) and fruit. It was used as a pie filling. Over the years, the meat content was reduced (or eliminated) and today it is more common to find a blend of nuts, dried fruit, raisins, apples, pears, or citrus peel with spices and brandy or rum.

FUN FOOD FACT
Victorian England revived the tradition of serving mincemeat as part of the Yuletide feast after it had gone out of style in most parts of Europe.

October 27
POTATO DAY

Despite being delicious either fried, baked, or boiled, the potato rarely gets the praise it deserves. While these root vegetables are synonymous with Ireland, they are actually indigenous to Peru. The Spanish conquistadors brought them back to Europe and began to cultivate them. Potatoes are cheap, very easy to grow, and do not require massive amounts of fertilizer or chemical additives to thrive. So enjoy your potato today, no matter how it is served.

{ *A woman poses in a pile of potatoes, ca. 1940s.*

FUN FOOD FACT

A potato blight in the 1840s caused the Great Famine in Ireland. Sadly, millions died and suffered greatly, as the working class relied heavily on potatoes as their main food staple. The famine caused mass waves of emigration from Ireland.

October 28
CHOLATE DAY

Chocolate is perhaps one of the best foods to celebrate today, with Americans consuming around ten pounds a year per person, in addition to half of the world's chocolate. We love chocolate! From chocolate candy bars to chocolate insects, nothing tastes bad covered in chocolate!

FUN FOOD FACT

Hershey's Kisses were first made in 1907 and were shaped as squares. A new machine changed the shape to a "kiss" in 1921.

{ *A woman eating chocolate, 1886.*

October 29
OATMEAL DAY

Oatmeal is one of the most common food items in American kitchens and has been around for centuries prior to the arrival of the early colonists. Oatmeal is made from hulled oat grains, or groats, that are either ground, called ground or white oats; steel-cut, called Irish oatmeal; or rolled, called old-fashioned, quick, or instant oatmeal. There are countless uses and recipes for oatmeal, from oatmeal-raisin cookies to classic porridges.

October 30
CANDY CORN DAY

Halloween just is not the same without some candy corn. George Renninger from Philadelphia, Pennsylvania, is claimed to have invented these colorful kernels in the 1880s. The Goelitz Confectionary Company (today named Jelly Belly Candy Co.) bought the rights in 1898 and continues to produce them. Candy corn was first called Chicken Feed, and the boxes featured a rooster with the slogan "Something Worth Crowing For." Interestingly, the candy was never intended to be marketed as a Halloween specialty, since trick-or-treating did not take off until the late 1940s.

October 31
CARAMEL APPLE DAY

Before there were caramel apples, there were candy apples, with William Kolb from Newark, New Jersey, claiming credit for their invention in 1908, while experimenting with cinnamon candy for the holiday season. He dipped an apple into the mixture and voilà, a classic was born. Skip ahead to the 1950s, to Dan Walker from Kraft Foods, who, while experimenting with ways to use up leftover caramel candies from Halloween, dipped an apple into a pot of melted caramel candies. The caramel apples were an immediate hit, and soon variations appeared using nuts and chocolate.

NOVEMBER

Food Celebrations This Month

National Fun with Fondue Month

National Georgia Pecan Month

National Peanut Butter Lover's Month

National Pepper Month

National Stuffing Month

National Raisin Bread Month

National Fig Week (November 1–7)

November 1
BISON DAY

The American bison, commonly referred to as the buffalo, is the national mammal of the United States. Of the eight known original species of bison—which descended from a south Asian ancestor and roamed the grasslands of Eurasia and North America as early as two million years ago—only the American bison and the eastern European wisent remain. Today, Yellowstone National Park is home to the oldest and largest bison herd, with nearly five thousand members. The nomadic Plains Indian tribes of North America centered their lives around the yearly migration patterns of bison. These animals became a sacred symbol of the Native American way of life because they were a source of food, shelter, clothing, weapons, spoons, rattles, and paintbrushes, and satisfied countless other needs.

{ *Two bison harnessed to a cart in (possibly) Butte, Montana, 1910.*

FUN FOOD FACT
Since the mid-nineteenth century, American bison and domestic cattle have been intentionally crossbred to produce the beefalo (also known as cattalo), which produces a superior meat that is lower in fat and cholesterol than regular beef.

November 2
DEVILED EGG DAY

In ancient Rome, eggs often were boiled, seasoned with spices, and served as appetizers to wealthy guests. Boiled eggs stuffed with flavored yolk mixtures were served in thirteenth-century Spain, but the term "deviled" did not emerge until 1786 in Great Britain, where it referred to food seasoned with hot spices. In Sweden, "stuffed eggs" with caviar and dill are commonly served as part of the annual Easter smorgasbord.

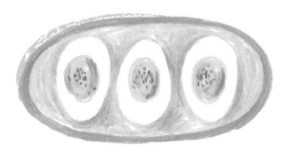

November 3
SANDWICH DAY

The word "sandwich" comes from the eighteenth-century gambling parlors of London, when John Montagu, the 4th Earl of Sandwich, insisted on eating meat between two pieces of bread in order to keep his hands clean during hours-long card games. Of course, the concept of placing ingredients between pieces of bread arose much earlier—at least as far back as the first century B.C., when the Jewish Rabbi Hillel the Elder began the Passover custom of wrapping meat and bitter herbs between soft matzah bread to symbolize the Hebrews' escape from their bitter existence in Egypt.

November 4
CANDY DAY

{ *An owner serving a customer at Bach Branch Office in Saint Louis, Missouri, 1910.*

Sugarcane was first cultivated in India and Southeast Asia around the sixth century B.C. Before that time, many ancient cultures made candy from honey. The first record of candy as a product of boiled sugarcane, known in India as *khanda*, comes from ancient Sanskrit texts. Before the Industrial Revolution, candy was often made of a combination of sugar and spices and intended for therapeutic use—such as calming the stomach. It was initially only available to the wealthy.

November 5
DOUGHNUT DAY

{ *A French infantryman surrounded by American soldiers while eating his first doughnut at an American Red Cross Canteen in Toul, France, 1918.*

Was this deep-fried American pastry invented by Dutch settlers, or by a sixteen-year-old aboard a lime-trading ship in 1847? One recent historian points to a circa-1800 "dow nuts" recipe described by Baroness Dimsdale of Hertford, England, in which sugar, eggs, butter, yeast, and nutmeg are combined and cut into "nuts," which are deep-fried in "hogs lard" and covered in sugar. Whatever their origin, these high-calorie snacks are quite addictive: North Carolina–based Krispy Kreme Doughnuts opened its one thousandth shop in 2015!

November 6
NACHOS DAY

Nachos were invented in the Mexican border town of Piedras Negras by Ignacio ("Nacho") Anaya when wives of U.S. soldiers stationed at nearby Fort Duncan arrived at his restaurant after it had closed. In a story resembling the spontaneous creation of the Caesar salad, Anaya worked with what he had left over that day, frying triangle-cut tortillas and covering them with shredded Cheddar cheese and pickled jalapeños. "Nacho's especiales" became a hit, to say the least, and his hometown now hosts a "biggest nacho in the world" contest every year in mid-October.

November 7
BITTERSWEET CHOCOLATE WITH ALMONDS DAY

Approximately 40 percent of the world's almonds are sold to chocolate manufacturers. In America, chocolate is considered bittersweet if it contains at least 70 percent cacao. A recipe for chocolate-covered almonds from the London cookbook *The Complete Housewife,* which was the first cookbook to be printed in the colonies, was the only chocolate recipe selected to appear in its printing in 1742. Each chocolate-covered almond contains an average of seventeen calories, two-thirds of which come from fat.

November 8
CAPPUCCINO DAY

The word "cappuccino" has its origins in the eighteenth-century coffee-houses of Vienna, where baristas began serving a drink called *Kapuziner*—referring to the brown robes of the Capuchin monks—that contained coffee, cream, and sugar. However, the modern drink we associate with the word was developed in the twentieth century, following the invention of the espresso machine in 1884. Cappuccino was unknown outside of Italy until 1930, and after World War II, the recipe was refined to include espresso as well as a mixture of steamed and frothed milk, which allow the drink to stay warm for longer periods of time.

November 9
GREEK YOGURT DAY

Greek yogurt is actually a Turkish invention. Anatolian goatherds first created yogurt in the third millennium B.C. by preserving fermented milk in sheepskin bags. In the second century A.D., the famous physician Galen wrote of a similar dairy product in Greece called *oxygala*, which, like the modern Greek-style (strained) yogurt, was often eaten with honey. Today, most yogurts contain the bacteria *Streptococcus thermophilus* and *Lactobacillus bulgaricus*, which are believed to help digestion and might explain why a Dr. Kellogg popularized yogurt-based enemas at Michigan's Battle Creek Sanitarium.

November 10
VANILLA CUPCAKE DAY

The first known American cookbook to be written in the colonies—*American Cookery* by Amelia Simms—was published in 1796 and contains the first mention of the cupcake, described as "a cake to be baked in small cups." Before the advent of muffin tins in the late nineteenth century, cupcakes were baked in actual cups, mugs, or ramekins. The fluted, thin, paper cupcake liners we are familiar with today became available after World War II, setting off a "cupcake craze" in the 1950s.

FUN FOOD FACT

While the original vanilla orchid vine was cultivated by Mesoamerican societies, today most of our vanilla comes from Madagascar, Réunion, and other islands of the Indian Ocean.

Vanilla Cupcakes

Makes 12 cupcakes

INGREDIENTS

2 cups all-purpose flour

2 teaspoons baking powder

½ teaspoon kosher salt

2 teaspoons vanilla extract

½ cup whole milk

½ cup (1 stick) butter, softened to room temperature

1 cup sugar

2 large eggs, at room temperature

DIRECTIONS

1. Preheat the oven to 375°F. Line a muffin pan with cupcake liners and set aside.

2. In a medium bowl, sift together the flour, baking powder, and salt.

3. In a small bowl, stir the vanilla into the milk.

4. Using an electric mixer on medium-high speed, cream the butter and sugar together until smooth and fluffy, 2 to 3 minutes. Add the eggs, mixing until light and creamy and scraping down the sides of the mixing bowl.

5. Add one-third of the dry ingredients, alternating with the liquid ingredients in three additions, beginning and ending with the wet ingredients.

6. Carefully scoop the batter into the muffin cups, filling each about three-quarters full.

7. Transfer the pan to the preheated oven and bake for 18 to 20 minutes or until the tops of the muffins spring back when lightly touched and a toothpick inserted in the center of the cupcakes comes out clean.

8. Let the cupcakes cool in the pan for 10 minutes before transferring them to a wire rack to cool completely. Top with your favorite frosting, if desired.

November 11
SUNDAE TOPPINGS DAY

When and where did the sundae originate? The jury is still out, but the state of Wisconsin is vehement that the dessert was born in the town of Two Rivers in 1881, when George Hallauer asked the owner of a soda fountain to top his ice cream with chocolate sauce. According to this account, this concoction was thereafter served every Sunday, but that soon changed when a ten-year-old girl came in one day and insisted on ice cream with "that stuff on top," even though it wasn't Sunday. And thus, the ice-cream-with-toppings trend began.

November 12
PIZZA WITH THE WORKS (EXCEPT ANCHOVIES) DAY

Predated by Italian *focaccia*, flatbread pizza did not emerge in Italy until after American tomatoes were brought to Europe in the 1600s. While many Europeans thought this nightshade fruit was poisonous, it became a popular topping for flatbread among the poor of Naples a century later. Today, many Italians prefer the simple *marinara* (tomato, oregano, garlic, olive oil) and *margherita* (tomato, mozzarella, basil) varieties, but in America after World War II it became common to add all sorts of toppings to pizza—mushrooms, olives, peppers, sausage, etc.—though anchovies are much less popular.

November 13
INDIAN PUDDING DAY

Indian pudding is really a misnomer for this New England dessert because Native Americans did not have the milk and molasses to create it. In reality, Indian pudding evolved from the English recipe for hasty pudding, which was made by boiling wheat flour in milk. The early American colonists adapted it by substituting cornmeal for wheat. Sweeteners like molasses and maple syrup, along with cinnamon or ginger, were also added. Now it's a cold-weather classic that is often served at Thanksgiving.

FUN FOOD FACT
American poet and diplomat Joel Barlow, feeling homesick for his native New England, penned a tribute to this colonial dessert in 1796.

November 14
GUACAMOLE DAY

The word "avocado" derives from the Nahuatl word *āhuacatl*, referring to the Mexican fruit (it's technically a large berry with a single seed). Fittingly, the Aztecs believed the green, fatty fruit was an aphrodisiac, and they combined it with onions, chiles, and tomatoes—much like the modern dip—calling the mixture *āhuacamolli*. Avocados have the highest fat content of any fruit, but they are associated with lower blood LDL cholesterol and triglyceride levels and are a great source of potassium and vitamin K. Here's to heart health!

November 15
RAISIN BRAN CEREAL DAY

Introduced in 1926, Skinner's Raisin Bran was the original raisin bran to hit the market in the United States. The now-familiar Kellogg's Raisin Bran entered the market in 1942, followed in 1966 by its mascot: a jovial, cartoon Sun named Sunny. The first dried, manufactured breakfast cereal in the world, Granula, was invented in 1863 by Dr. James Caleb Jackson, an American abolitionist and hydrotherapy advocate who ran a spa called Our Home on the Hillside in Dansville, New York. In 2016, Kellogg announced it would release a new line of raisin bran granola in response to the growing trend among millennials of substituting granola and yogurt for cereal and other snacks.

{ *Portrait of John Harvey Kellogg, 1913.*

November 16
FAST FOOD DAY

According to the National Restaurant Association, American sales of fast food totaled $163.5 billion in 2005. Drive-through windows have existed since the 1930s, but the familiar speaker system used to place orders wasn't around until the 1950s.

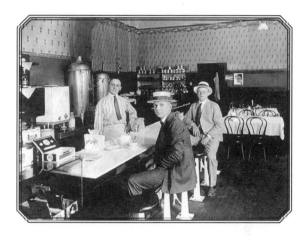

{ *A coffee shop, ca. 1920–30.*

November 17
HOMEMADE BREAD DAY

{ *Men waiting for bread in a breadline in the Bowery neighborhood of New York City, 1910.*

How long has bread been around? No one really knows, but preserved bread loaves excavated from Old Kingdom tombs suggest that the ancient Egyptians used a labor-intensive process to grind emmer wheat into flour, which was in turn combined with water and baked within molds on hearth embers. According to Pliny the Elder, people living in the regions of present-day France and Spain used beer foam as a leavening agent in the first century. In recent years, bread has been demonized by the church of Atkins and the paleo-diet movement, but no one can deny its role in the rise of human societies.

November 18
APPLE CIDER DAY

Chibble's Wilding, Kentish Fill-Basket, Hangdown—these are just a few of the colorful names for apple varieties used in the production of cider. This drink was made and imbibed in England during ancient Roman times, and during the calamitous fourteenth century, English priests are believed to have substituted cider for water during baptisms in order to keep pestilence at bay. Nowadays, the beverage is strongly associated with major autumn holidays and often served mulled and heated.

November 19
MACCHIATO DAY

The word "macchiato" literally means "stained" or "spotted" in Italian and thus refers to espressos that have been "stained" or "spotted" with foamed milk. The drink is served everywhere from Ethiopia to Thailand, and in Mexico the term *cortado* (diluted) is sometimes used, although—confusingly—the term also refers to a milkier coffee drink popular throughout Latin America.

FUN FOOD FACT
The macchiato has the highest espresso-to-milk ratio of any coffee drink with those ingredients.

November 20
PEANUT-BUTTER FUDGE DAY

W hen and where was peanut butter fudge invented? No one knows for sure, but fudge is probably an American invention from the 1880s. At the time, the word fudge referred to a "hoax" or "error." Some believe the first batch of this crystalline sugar-butter-milk mixture was created from a "fudged" batch of caramels. The name stuck. Today, the most popular fudge flavor is chocolate, but the substitution of peanut butter for cocoa provides some healthy extra fiber and protein.

FUN FOOD FACT

Krówki *(literally, "little cows"), which has a solid outer layer and creamy filling, is a popular version of fudge from Poland.*

November 21
GINGERBREAD COOKIE DAY

The art of making gingerbread may have been brought to Europe in 992 A.D., after the Persian army chased the Armenian archbishop Gregory Makar from Nicopolis (modern-day Greece) to France's Loire Valley, near the town of Pithiviers. There, he introduced his native land's honey and spice cakes to local Christians. Rumor has it that a medieval Copenhagen pharmacy sent King Hans of Scandinavia (1455–1513) several pounds of gingerbread as a cure for his depression. Royals such as Emperor Frederick III hired skilled artisans to fashion intricate cookie molds for gingerbread that could be distributed as propaganda. Catholic monks used to make gingerbread in the shape of angels and saints—a tradition adapted from the pagan Germanic custom of offering "picture cookies" in the shape of horses to Nordic gods during the winter solstice celebration.

November 22
CRANBERRY RELISH DAY

A regular accompaniment to the traditional Thanksgiving meal, cranberry relish is probably derived from the British barberry conserve—a sour fruit and sugar stew often served with meat. Cranberries are native to North America and were traditionally used by Native Americans for medicinal and dietary purposes, as well as for dyes. They combined cranberries with dried meat and animal fat, creating pemmican—a food that sustained many fur traders and their dogs on the harsh Canadian frontier. Today, Americans consume more than five million gallons of canned, jellied cranberry sauce "logs" every Holiday season, which were introduced by Ocean Spray in 1941.

{ *Workers gathering cranberries from the surface of a flooded bog in Burlington County, New Jersey, 1938.*

Orange Cranberry Relish

Makes 2½ cups

INGREDIENTS

½ orange (with skin), cut into 6
  pieces and seeded
12 ounces cranberries
2 tablespoons raspberry jam
3 tablespoons sugar

DIRECTIONS

1. Place the orange pieces in a food processor. Pulse until chopped into pea-sized pieces. Add the cranberries and pulse until finely chopped.

2. Transfer the cranberry mixture to a medium bowl, and whisk in the raspberry jam and sugar. Stir until the jam is incorporated and the sugar is dissolved.

3. Refrigerate relish for 1 hour to allow the flavors to develop and the sugar to dissolve completely. Use immediately or store in the refrigerator for about a week.

November 23
ESPRESSO DAY

{ *An Italian-American cafe and shop on MacDougal Street in Little Italy, New York City, ca. 1942.*

The term "espresso" refers to a beverage as well as a brewing method in which a small amount of very hot water is forced through ground coffee beans, resulting in a thick, highly concentrated coffee drink. The steam-driven espresso machine was invented by Angelo Moriondo in Italy in 1884. Various engineers improved on the device over the ensuing decades, and now artisanal espresso bars have sprung up all over the world.

November 24
SARDINES DAY

Related to herring, sardines are small, vitamin-rich, oily fish commonly packaged in cans. The term "sardine" probably comes from the Mediterranean island of Sardinia, where the fish were abundant in the fifteenth century. They were also a major dietary staple among the ancient Norte Chico civilization of Peru. Sardines contain high levels of vitamin B-12, vitamin D, calcium, and omega-3 fatty acids, so nutritionists consider them one of the healthiest foods available.

FUN FOOD FACT
Sardines are low enough in the food chain that they have much lower levels of mercury contamination than larger fish like the tuna.

November 25
PARFAIT DAY

Parfait is the French word for "perfect," and it's no wonder. Though originally used to describe both sweet and savory layered dishes, the term in America has been associated with desserts served in tall glasses and consisting of layers of ice cream or yogurt layered with fruit, granola, nuts, and syrups of various kinds. The traditional French dessert version, by contrast, usually takes the form of a frozen custard made from boiled cream, egg, and sugar. The United Kingdom has its own take on the parfait, as well, mixing duck liver paste with sweet liqueurs.

November 26
CAKE DAY

"Let them eat cake!" exclaimed Marie Antoinette upon learning of the bread shortage among the French peasantry (according to legend, anyway). In ancient Roman times, the addition of eggs, honey, and butter gave bread its familiar sweetness and crumbly consistency. The more down-to-earth Scots used the term "cake" to refer to thick, hard oatmeal biscuits, and from the seventeenth to nineteenth centuries, Scotland was humorously known as the "Land of Cakes." In fact, the Scottish New Year's holiday, known as Hogmanay, was also called "Cake Day" after the confections given to local children who knocked on their neighbors' doors.

{ *A cake contest, 1938.*

Hot Milk Bundt Cake

Makes 16 servings

INGREDIENTS

½ cup (1 stick) unsalted butter
1 cup whole milk
2 teaspoons vanilla extract
2 cups all-purpose flour
2 teaspoons baking powder
1 teaspoon kosher salt
4 eggs, at room temperature
2 cups sugar
Zest of 1 lemon

DIRECTIONS

1. Preheat the oven to 325°F. Grease and flour a standard Bundt cake pan.

2. In a medium saucepan over low heat, melt the butter. Stir in the milk and heat until the mixture is hot but not boiling. Turn off the heat and add the vanilla.

3. In a large bowl, sift together the flour, baking powder, and salt.

4. In a separate large bowl, using a handheld mixer fitted with the whisk attachment, beat the eggs, sugar, and lemon zest on medium speed until light and thickened, 4 to 5 minutes.

5. Once the egg and sugar mixture triples in volume, slowly add the milk mixture. Mix on low until completely combined.

6. Slowly add the dry ingredients to the wet ingredients, mixing after each addition until incorporated.

7. Pour the batter into the prepared pan and bake for 1 hour, or until a toothpick inserted in the center of the cake comes out clean. Make sure not to overbake.

8. Let cake cool in the pan for 10 minutes before inverting onto a cooling rack to cool completely.

November 27
BAVARIAN CREAM PIE DAY

Bavarian cream was originally a cold dessert of egg custard stiffened with gelatin and mixed with whipped cream. It has often been flavored with liqueurs, topped with fruit, and used as a filling for cakes and pastries. Before the advent of refrigeration, preparing Bavarian cream required dunking an airtight mold of the preparation in a salted, ice-filled bowl, much like Italian panna cotta. True Bavarian cream recipes first appeared in America in the late nineteenth century, beginning with *Mrs. Lincoln's Boston Cook Book*, which was published in 1884.

November 28
FRENCH TOAST DAY

French toast was invented in fourth-century A.D. Rome, as indicated by the Fulda monastery's *Apicius* cookbook. It was popular in the medieval period, and the French referred to the dish as *pain perdu* ("lost bread"), since the recipe provided an excellent way to salvage stale bread. Over the years, it has been called "Roman bread," "Spanish toast," and even "American toast," but the term we are familiar with today probably stuck because it was popularized in the United States by French immigrants.

FUN FOOD FACT
The Spanish torrija, created by soaking stale bread in milk or wine with honey and spices and then coating it in egg and frying it in olive oil, is a delicious version of French toast traditionally prepared for Lent.

November 29
CHOCOLATES DAY

Chocolate comes from the Aztec word *xocolatl*, which means "bitter water" and refers to the bitter taste of raw cocoa beans. Switzerland is the top global consumer of chocolate, with almost twenty pounds of chocolate consumed per person per year. Cocoa beans were used as currency by the Mayan and Aztec cultures prior to the Spanish conquest. (Maybe money really *does* grow on trees?) "Dutched" chocolate—the basis of modern hot cocoa, chocolates, and ice creams—was invented by the chemist Coenraad Johannes van Houten and his father in the early 1800s, when they developed a method for removing fat from roasted cocoa beans with a hydraulic press and then treating cocoa powder with alkaline salts to remove the bitter taste and darken its color.

November 30
MOUSSE DAY

Mousse is a French word meaning "froth" or "foam," and it refers to this dessert's unique light, frothy texture. The first known recipe for the popular mousse au chocolat appeared in a 1749 cookbook titled *La Science du Maître d'Hôtel Cuisineur* (roughly, *The Science of a Master Confectioner*) by the pseudonymous author Menon. In 1892, the term "chocolate mousse" finally arrived in the United States after the dish was presented at a food exposition held at Madison Square Garden in New York City.

FUN FOOD FACT
Savory mousses incorporate such foods as salmon, foie gras, and cheese, and they can be served atop an endless variety of prepared dishes.

winter

Food Celebrations This Month

National Eggnog Month

National Fruitcake Month

December 1
FRIED PIE DAY

A sort of cross between a regular pie and a turnover, fried pies are a specialty from the South, where they were first known as "crab lanterns"—perhaps because of their resemblance to crab apple pies that used slits to ventilate the steam. Some pie purists do not recognize fried pies as true pies, since they are fried, not baked, but whichever side of the pie debate you're on, really, what could be better than fried pie dough filled with fruit?

FUN FOOD FACT
McDonald's first introduced fried apple pies to its menu in 1968, but they were replaced in 1992 with a healthier baked version.

December 2
FRITTERS DAY

Although the term "fritter" can apply to many foods, it is usually used to describe a fried food made from a batter of either flour or cornmeal, eggs, and milk. Here in the United States, corn and apple fritters as well as hushpuppies are among the most popular fritters.

December 3
PEPPERMINT LATTE DAY

Café con leche, caffè latte, or café au lait . . . with so many terms referring to coffee and milk, it is no wonder that coffee, name confusion occurs daily across the United States. Coffee and milk have been a European breakfast staple for hundreds of years, but when the first espresso machine was invented by Angelo Moriondo in 1884, various espresso drinks became popular across Europe. Traditionally speaking, a latte is made with espresso and steamed milk and lightly topped with milk foam; however, nowadays it can be made with any type of coffee or tea—in addition to flavorings, such as today's ingredient, peppermint!

FUN FOOD FACTS
Cappuccinos *were invented in Austria in the early nineteenth century and were called* Kapuziner, *which translates to* cappuccino *in Italian.*

Cappuccinos *differ from* lattes *in that there is more milk foam than a* latte, *and they usually have spices, the most common being cinnamon.*

December 4
COOKIE DAY

As Americans, we simply cannot get enough cookies: We consume around three hundred per person per year, whether chocolate chip, oatmeal, snickerdoodle, or peanut butter. There is even a National Cookie Cutter Museum in Joplin, Missouri. So grab a bag of your favorite cookies or bake a batch and enjoy a cookie today!

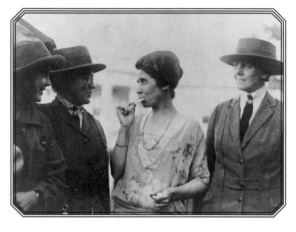

{ *Mrs. Coolidge eating cookies presented by a New York Girl Scout troop, 1923.*

FUN FOOD FACT
American cookie jars became popular during the Depression in the 1930s, when homemakers began baking cookies at home instead of buying them.

Red Velvet Butter Cookies

Makes 30 cookies

INGREDIENTS

2¼ cups all-purpose flour

3 tablespoons unsweetened cocoa powder

3 teaspoons baking powder

½ teaspoon kosher salt

8 ounces cream cheese, at room temperature

½ cup (1 stick) unsalted butter, at room temperature

1 cup granulated sugar

¾ cup packed light brown sugar

2 large eggs

1 tablespoon red food coloring

½ cup powdered sugar

DIRECTIONS

1. In a large bowl, whisk together the flour, cocoa, baking powder, and salt. Set aside.

2. In a separate large bowl, with a handheld mixer on medium speed, cream the cream cheese and butter with the sugars until light and fluffy, 2 to 3 minutes. Add the eggs and food coloring and continue beating on medium speed for 2 minutes longer.

3. Add the dry ingredients to wet ingredients and blend on medium speed until a dough forms, 1 to 2 minutes. (The dough will be very sticky.) Cover and refrigerate at least 2 hours or up to overnight.

4. When ready to bake, preheat the oven to 325°F. Line 2 baking sheets with parchment paper. Pour the powdered sugar into a small bowl. Set aside.

5. Once the dough has chilled, scoop the cookie dough with a small cookie scoop or generous tablespoon and roll dough between your palms to form a ball. Roll each ball in powdered sugar and place the cookies 2 inches apart on the prepared baking sheets.

6. Transfer the baking sheets to the preheated oven and bake for 10 to 14 minutes, and then transfer cookies to a wire rack to cool completely.

December 5
COMFORT FOOD DAY

Traced back to its first use in a 1966 *Palm Beach Post* article, the term "comfort food" was officially added to the *Oxford English Dictionary* in 1997. To some people, comfort food is a big plate of macaroni and cheese, while to others it is a hot bowl of ramen noodles. Comfort food brings us back to our roots, when we need that extra little something to calm our nerves or to lift our spirits when we are feeling down and blue. No matter what one's nostalgic dish is, today we celebrate every comfort food.

December 6
GAZPACHO DAY

Chilled soup? Who would have thought of such a concept? Well, the Spaniards did, and they named it *gazpacho*. Derived from the Latin word *caspa*, meaning "fragments or little pieces," gazpacho has been enjoyed for centuries in the southern Spanish region of Andalucía, where the temperatures can easily exceed one hundred degrees in the summer. However, it was not until the early Spanish explorers returned to Spain in the late fifteenth century with the first tomatoes did this New World food become gazpacho's signature ingredient. Like many simple rustic dishes there are countless variations of gazpacho, with each household and restaurant claiming its own signature style. The most common recipes call for tomatoes, garlic, vinegar, bread, and olive oil.

December 7
FAIRY FLOSS DAY

Fairy floss, which is the Australian term for cotton candy, has been around since the early twentieth century when it was introduced at the 1904 World's Fair by dentist William Morrison. Usually sold as either blue or pink, there are many flavors these days, such as raspberry, vanilla, watermelon, and even chocolate.

December 8
BROWNIE DAY

Brownies are wonderful little creations—so much so that we have several days celebrating these American treats. While the brownie has a few competing origin stories, many say it was a wealthy Chicago socialite who first created the dense chocolate squares. Whether consumed as part of a sundae, dipped into a chocolate fondue, or adapted to be a blondie (which is a brownie made with vanilla instead of chocolate), enjoy some brownies today!

December 9
PASTRY DAY

A private mixing pastry dough for thousands
of "doughboys" (a nickname for U.S. Army and
Marine Corps during World War I) waiting to
go home at the American Red Cross "Doughnut
Foundry" at Le Mans, France, 1919.

From cannolis and strudels to éclairs and tarts, pastries come in all kinds of flavors, sizes, and shapes, and life without these sweet indulgences would be pretty dull. The history of pastry is expansive, depending on the type of pastry and its country of origin, but we do know that the basics of pastry making were practiced by the ancient Greeks and Romans, both of whom used oil as a base. During later centuries, butter would replace oil as the main fat in pastry.

FUN FOOD FACT
Puff pastries "puff up" when baked because the water and fats from the butter turn into steam as the pastry is warmed, causing the layers to expand, resulting in an airy, flaky, and delicious treat.

December 10
LAGER DAY

{ *A cowboy drinking beer at a beer parlor in Alpine, Texas, 1939.*

Ale, pale ale, lager . . . there seem to be so many names for beer. However, each has its own unique style, flavor, and process, which gives us so many enjoyable varieties. The main difference between lager and ale is the temperature at which each is fermented. Usually, most brewers want their beer to convert to sugar gradually in a process called attenuation. The common yeast *Saccharomyces cerevisiae* (also called "top fermenting" or "ale" yeast) is used for ales and has a high tolerance to alcohol, which during fermentation creates a finished ale that is high in alcohol content. *Saccharomyces uvarum* (also called "bottom fermenting" or "lager" yeast) is used for lagers. It is much more fragile than ale yeast and causes the beer to attenuate slowly, giving lagers more body and crispness and less fruitiness than ales.

December 11
"HAVE A BAGEL" DAY

What could better for a Saturday morning breakfast than a perfectly toasted bagel with a smear of cream cheese? Arriving with Jewish immigrants in the late nineteenth century, bagels are the official New York City breakfast choice for millions. Although not technically a bagel, bialys are similar to their bagel cousins except they are not boiled, and in place of a hole, they have an onion, garlic, or poppy seed mixture in the middle.

FUN FOOD FACT
Montreal bagels are fantastic, too. They are smaller, denser, and sweeter than New York bagels. They are also usually not toasted.

December 12
AMBROSIA DAY

Is it a dessert or a salad? Do we eat it before or after a meal? These are some of the common questions that the Southern specialty ambrosia salad provokes. Derived from Greek and Roman mythology, ambrosia was the food of the gods, and the first mention of this sweet delight is in *Dixie Cookery* by Maria Massey Barringer in 1867. First made with oranges, grated coconut, and sugar, numerous ingredients have been added throughout the years, including marshmallows, Maraschino cherries, and whipped cream, to name a few.

Ambrosia Salad

Makes 6 servings

INGREDIENTS

1 (20-ounce) can pineapple chunks, drained

1 (11-ounce) can peaches, chopped and drained

1 (12-ounce) jar maraschino cherries, drained

2 green apples, peeled, cored and chopped

1 cup sweetened coconut flakes, toasted

2 cups Cool Whip, thawed

6 ounce plain Greek yogurt

1 cup miniature marshmallows

DIRECTIONS

1. Place the fruit and coconut flakes in a large serving bowl. Toss to combine.

2. In a separate bowl, whisk together the Cool Whip and yogurt. Pour over the fruit.

3. Add the marshmallows to the bowl and fold everything together with a spatula until combined.

4. Cover and chill at least 2 hours before serving.

December 13
POPCORN STRING DAY

A favorite Christmas decoration for trees and the home, garlands of popcorn strings trace their origins to the early 1800s, when Christmas décor was edible and included apples and nuts. After a while, paper streamers began to be included. Soon, Americans began to add popcorn and cranberries.

FUN FOOD FACT
Bird lovers have gotten very creative with the "edible garland" concept, creating strings of everything from Cheerios, to dried orange slices, to festively shaped stale bread for their feathered friends to enjoy out of doors.

December 14
BISQUITS & GRAVY DAY

Yet one more classic Southern dish, biscuits and gravy became iconic after the Revolutionary War, when supplies and food were scarce and a cheap, but fulfilling breakfast was needed to keep farmers nourished for the hard day's work. As usual, there are many variations of biscuits and gravy, but the main ingredients usually consist of biscuits covered in a sausage gravy made from flour, milk (or buttermilk), and meat drippings.

December 15
LEMON CUPCAKE DAY

Cupcakes continue to be a national craze, with whole franchises dedicated to these wonderful minidesserts. With a couple of cupcake days to celebrate, today is all about lemon! The tart and sweet flavors of a lemon cupcake are perfect with a delicious buttercream frosting.

FUN FOOD FACT

Although it does contain citral, the same essential oil found in lemons have, lemongrass is not related to lemons.

December 16
CHOCOLATE-COVERED EVERYTHING DAY

Chocolate ganache was invented in the 1850s and is made by pouring heated cream over chopped chocolate to create a multipurpose glaze and icing. Butter is also often added to give a shiny appearance.

FUN FOOD FACT

For those of you with a taste for the exotic, chocolate-covered roasted crickets are sold online and considered a delicacy in countries like Thailand.

December 17
MAPLE SYRUP DAY

Taken from the sap of three species of maple trees, maple syrup was used by Northeastern Native Americans long before the arrival of the early colonists. Some tribes used the sap as a drink while others preferred to cook with it. After the Native Americans taught the settlers how to harvest the sap, maple syrup became a staple sweetener for hot cereals, breads, and, of course, pancakes.

{ *A worker gathering sap from trees to make maple syrup in North Bridgewater, Vermont, ca. 1940.*

FUN FOOD FACTS

Today, Canada produces more than 80 percent of the world's maple syrup.

In protest of the slave labor involved in creating molasses and cane sugar, American Civil War abolitionists stuck to maple syrup as their preferred sweetener.

December 18
"I LOVE HONEY" DAY

{ *A honeycomb being lifted from a hive at the Bethlehem Poultry Farm in Bethlehem, West Bank, 1939.*

With evidence dating back eight thousand years ago to cave paintings in Valencia, Spain, humans have depended on busy bees and their sweet creation for millennia. The ancient Egyptians used honey as a sweetener as well as for embalming the dead, and for the ancient Greeks and Romans, it was their most important sweetener, since they did not have sugar. In addition to its culinary uses, honey was also used for medicinal purposes throughout history. No matter the application, honey is one treasured ingredient.

December 19
OATMEAL MUFFIN DAY

Combine one of America's favorite morning quick breads with another cherished hot cereal and we get today's celebratory food, the oatmeal muffin. Derived from the German word *Muffin*, meaning "small cake," muffins have been around since early 1700s.

FUN FOOD FACT
Cedar Rapids, Iowa, produces the most oats in the United States.

December 20
SANGRIA DAY

Reaching the American palate at the 1964 World's Fair in New York, *sangria*—which is similar to a punch—has been a festive and popular drink ever since. Although there are many varieties using different combinations of fruits and wine, the basic sangria recipe calls for red wine, fruit juice, soda water, fruit, and brandy.

FUN FOOD FACT
When white wine is used in sangria, it is called sangria blanca.

December 21
FRIED SHRIMP DAY

Shrimp, batter, and frying . . . what could possibly be wrong with this equation? Americans eat more shrimp than any other seafood—not to mention our love for anything fried—so it is no wonder that we love fried shrimp, which surfaced on restaurant menus in the early twentieth century. After World War II, breaded, deep-fried shrimp quickly shot up in popularity, due to the availability of precooked frozen shrimp.

FUN FOOD FACT
Some claim that Red Lobster invented popcorn shrimp in 1974.

December 22
DATE NUT BREAD DAY

Believed to have been first cultivated in Iraq, dates have served as a staple food for centuries. Dates were introduced to North America by the Spaniards, when they arrived in Mexico and California. These delicious fruits are used in many ways, including chutney, baked goods (like today's celebrated food), and even as a vinegar.

FUN FOOD FACT
Medjool dates, originally from Morocco, were brought to the United States in 1927, quarantined for seven years, and then planted in Southern California in 1944.

December 23
BAKE DAY

{ *A woman selling baked goods by the roadside, ca. 1925–30.*

Cooks and bakers, get the pans out and start baking! The holidays are quickly approaching and the countdown has begun. Whether classic gingerbread or sugar cookies, chocolate or caramel fudge, or macaroons, celebrate all that is baked today!

FUN FOOD FACT

The practice of leaving milk and cookies out for Santa Claus began during the Great Depression in the 1930s as a way to teach children how to share during difficult times.

December 24
EGGNOG DAY

Believe it or not, eggnog is actually a custard! Dating to the late seventeenth century, "nog" referred to beer that was brewed in East Anglia, England, and a "noggin" was a small cup used to drink nog. Many food historians think today's version came from a thick medieval drink called *posset* that was made from hot milk, liquor, and spices. The early colonists particularly enjoyed egg-based drinks due to the abundance of milk, eggs, and rum.

{ *A wood-engraved illustration from* Harper's Weekly, *December 31, 1870, depicting an eggnog party during a Southern U.S. Christmas party, drawn by W. L. Sheppard.*

FUN FOOD FACT
Traditional eggnog recipes used rum, which was readily available to the colonists, but nowadays, bourbon is the preferred choice.

December 25
PUMPKIN PIE DAY

{ *Workers gathering pumpkins in Yakima Valley, Washington, 1904.*

FUN FOOD FACT

In England, pumpkins were first called pumpions, after the French word pompon, meaning "bobble," since they had a round form.

A classic holiday dish that every American knows well, pumpkin pie is a definite favorite. Native to Central America and cultivated since 5500 B.C., pumpkins and squash were one of the first foods to be brought back to Europe after the New World was discovered. The English were very adept at making pies. By the time the Pilgrims landed at Plymouth Rock, food historians think that they would have been familiar with pumpkin and would have applied their pie-making skills to the new foods they encountered. Early versions of pumpkin pie differed greatly from those of today. Seventeenth-century French cookbooks recommended boiling the pumpkin in milk, straining it, and then adding it to the piecrust. There are a couple of pumpkin pie recipes in Amelia Simmon's 1796 cookbook *American Cookery*, the first known cookbook produced in the colonies, one of which is a custard variation similar to today's version.

Pumpkin Pie Minicakes

Makes 12 minicakes

INGREDIENTS

1 (15-ounce) can pumpkin purée
½ cup granulated sugar
¼ cup packed light brown sugar
2 large eggs
1 teaspoon vanilla extract
¾ cup sweetened condensed milk
⅔ cup almond meal (or flour)
2 teaspoons pumpkin pie spice
¼ teaspoon kosher salt
¼ teaspoon baking powder
¼ teaspoon baking soda
Powdered sugar

DIRECTIONS

1. Preheat the oven to 350°F. Line a 12-cup muffin pan with liners and set aside.

2. In a large bowl, whisk together the pumpkin purée, granulated sugar, brown sugar, eggs, vanilla, and condensed milk. Set aside.

3. In another large bowl, whisk together the almond meal (or flour), pumpkin pie spice, salt, baking powder, and baking soda.

4. Add the dry ingredients to the wet ingredients and mix with a wooden spoon until just combined; do not overmix.

5. Fill each cup with ⅓ cup batter. Transfer the pan to the preheated oven and bake for 20 minutes or until the cakes spring back when lightly touched.

6. Remove from the oven and cool in the pan for 5 minutes before removing from the pan and allowing to cool completely. Dust each minicake with powdered sugar.

December 26
CANDY CANE DAY

Tradition has it that candy canes were first invented in 1670 by a choirmaster at the Cologne Cathedral in Germany, when he asked a candy maker to create a treat to cccupy children while the Nativity scene was performed during the Christmas Eve mass. The crook at the top was meant to represent the shepherds who came to visit the baby Jesus. The tradition spread from Germany throughout Europe. Here in the United States, August Imgard, a German immigrant, is credited with introducing candy canes to Americans in Wooster, Ohio. Bob McCormack began making candy canes for his children in the 1920s, and with the help of his brother-in-law, a Catholic priest named Gregory Harding Keller, started to mass produce them under the name Bobs Candies. Their candy cane machine to bend the tops is called the Keller Machine.

FUN FOOD FACT

Of the 1.2 billion candy canes made each year, 90 percent are consumed between Thanksgiving and Christmas.

December 27
FRUITCAKE DAY

Either beloved or hated, fruitcakes have been with us since ancient Roman times. The precursor to today's version consisted of barley, pomegranate seeds, and nuts. By the Middle Ages, dried fruits began to be added, with different countries adopting their own versions, such as *panaforte* in Italy, *stollen* in Germany, and *black cake* in the Caribbean. By the nineteenth century, fruitcakes became popular choices for weddings and the holidays.

December 28
BOXED CHOCOLATES DAY

Wrapped in foil, boxed chocolates are a thing of beauty. Richard Cadbury, whose family produced chocolate in England, is credited with making "eating chocolates" instead of using chocolate in liquid form. Here in the United States, the Russell Stover Company began manufacturing chocolate in Denver, Colorado, in 1923. Whitman's chocolate, which was started in 1842 by Stephen F. Whitman in Philadelphia, Pennsylvania, was bought by Russell Stover in 1993.

December 29
PEPPER POT DAY

Consisting of a thick and hearty stew made of beef tripe and vegetables, pepper pot is an old dish, dating back to the Revolutionary War, when soldiers in the Continental Army, camping near Valley Forge, Pennsylvania, survived the harsh winter on this dish.

FUN FOOD FACT

The Campbell Soup Company sold canned pepper pot soup for more than one hundred years before stopping production in 2010.

December 30
BAKING SODA DAY

Known also as bicarbonate of soda, bread soda, and cooking soda, baking soda has been used for thousands of years in so many ways. In 1846, John Dwight and Austin Church developed baking soda to be used as leavening agent and called their company Arm & Hammer. Prior to this time, cooks had to rely on potash to make baked goods lighter. When baking soda is mixed with an acid, such as lemon juice, vinegar, sour milk, or cream of tartar, it creates gas bubbles, creating the leavening effect.

December 31
CHAMPAGNE DAY

Whether it's for weddings, birthdays, or New Year's Eve, champagne is synonymous with anything worth celebrating! In the purest sense, champagne is a sparkling wine that comes from the Champagne region of northwestern France, where the climate creates superb grapes. Champagne begins like most wines, but then undergoes a process called *Méthode Champenoise*, which adds yeast and sugar to the previously fermented wine, giving champagne its signature bubbles.

FUN FOOD FACT

Benedictine monk Dom Pierre Pérignon, a cellar master, is credited with creating champagne in the seventeenth century when he discovered bubbles in his wine, which resulted from a change of weather. To fix it, he blended grapes. Legend states that after tasting the first champagne, he declared to his fellow monks, "Come quickly, brothers. I'm tasting stars!"

cream

January

Food Celebrations This Month

National Hot Tea Month

National Oatmeal Month

National Slow Cooking Month

National Soup Month

National Baking Month

National Fat-Free Living Month

January 1
BLOODY MARY DAY

The Bloody Mary has been called "the world's most complex cocktail" and it was likely invented in 1921 by bartender Fernand "Pete" Petiot at Harry's New York Bar in Paris, France, a hangout for numerous famous American expats such as Sinclair Lewis, Ernest Hemingway, Jack Dempsey, Rita Hayworth, and Humphrey Bogart. Originally named the Red Snapper, the Bloody Mary was first mixed with either gin or vodka.

FUN FOOD FACT
Besides its famous clientele, the landmark bar Harry's can also proudly boast to being the birthplace of several other classic cocktails: the French 75, the Sidecar, and the Monkey Gland. Inside, at the "Ivories" Piano Bar, George Gershwin composed "An American in Paris."

Bloody Mary

Makes 1 drink

INGREDIENTS

2 ounces vodka

4 ounces tomato juice

1 dash lime juice

3 dashes celery salt

1 teaspoon prepared horseradish

2 dashes coarse black pepper

2 dashes cayenne pepper

4 dashes Worcestershire sauce

2 dashes hot pepper sauce

Celery, for garnish

DIRECTIONS

1. Place all ingredients in glass, stir, and serve over ice. Garnish with celery.

January 2
CREAM PUFF DAY

Considered a type of profiterole, cream puffs are small, round, filled pastries. In French, they are called *choux à la crème*, meaning "little cabbage filled with cream." Many say cream puffs were invented by the cook of Catherine de Medici. The cream puff first appeared on American restaurant menus around 1850.

FUN FOOD FACT
The record for the world's largest cream puff was set at the 2011 Wisconsin State Fair. It weighed in at 125.5 pounds.

January 3
CHOCOLATE-COVERED CHERRY DAY

Who doesn't love cherries? Cherries were brought to North America in the 1600s by the early settlers. Today cherry-pie filling is the number-one pie filling sold in the United States. Interestingly, darker cherries have a higher level of antioxidants and vitamins than lighter-colored ones. To punch up the delectable taste of cherries even more, today we cover them in chocolate to bring them to a whole new level!

Dark Chocolate–Covered Cherries

Makes 60

INGREDIENTS

3 tablespoons unsalted butter, at room temperature

3 tablespoons light corn syrup

2 cups powdered sugar, sifted

60 Maraschino cherries with stems, drained and patted dry

1½ cup dark chocolate chips

2 teaspoons vegetable oil

DIRECTIONS

1. In a medium bowl with a handheld mixer on medium speed, cream the butter and corn syrup for 1 minute. Stir in the powdered sugar with a wooden spoon; a light dough will form.

2. Cover the bowl with plastic wrap and chill in the freezer for 10 minutes to stiffen.

3. After the dough has chilled, wrap each cherry with 1 teaspoon of the mixture. Arrange the covered cherries on a parchment paper–lined baking sheet and transfer to the freezer to chill again until firm, 15 to 20 minutes.

4. In a microwave-safe bowl, heat the dark chocolate and oil in the microwave in 20-second intervals, stirring after every interval, until the chocolate is evenly melted and smooth, about 1 minute total.

5. Dip each frozen covered cherry into the chocolate mixture holding it by its stem and place on a parchment paper–lined baking sheet to set, about 1 hour in a cool place. Serve when the chocolate is set.

January 4
SPAGHETTI DAY

Spaghetti is one those dishes that almost every culture has adopted in some shape or form. In Italy, pasta is an art form, with the average Italian eating more than fifty-one pounds of it every year. The Italian word *spaghetti* is the plural form of the singular *spaghetto*, meaning "thin string" or "twine." On a curious note, even though pasta has existed for thousands of years, tomatoes were not introduced to the dish until the 1500s. According to Miss Manners (aka Judith Martin), a fork is the only utensil that may be used to eat spaghetti "while anyone is looking," but according to Foodimentary.com, one can do it however one likes.

FUN FOOD FACT

Thomas Jefferson is credited with being the first person to introduce pasta to America in 1789.

January 5
WHIPPED CREAM DAY

Believe it or not, whipped cream was popular way back in the sixteenth century, when it was referred to as "milk snow" and "snow cream." An English recipe from 1545 suggested flavoring whipped egg whites with rosewater and sugar, but lacking modern electric mixers, cooks were forced to use willow and rush branches to create the frothy texture. Crème Chantilly is another term often used to refer to this fluffy topping, though it only came into popular use in the nineteenth century.

January 6
SHORTBREAD DAY

Shortbread may have been made as early as the twelfth century; however, its invention is often attributed to Mary, Queen of Scots, in the sixteenth century. It is said that the queen enjoyed a traditional form of shortbread called petticoat tails, which was flavored with caraway seeds, baked, and cut into triangular wedges. Scottish shortbread evolved from medieval biscuit bread, which was a twice-baked, enriched bread roll dusted with sugar and spices and then hardened. Eventually, butter was substituted for yeast, and shortbread was born. Since butter was such an important ingredient, the word "shortbread" derived from "shortening."

January 7
TEMPURA DAY

It is believed that tempura was introduced to Japan in the mid-sixteenth century by Portuguese Jesuits. Interestingly, it is during this same period that *panko* and *tonkatsu* were also introduced from Portugal. The word *tempura* is derived from the Latin word *tempora*, meaning "times" or "time period," which both Spanish and Portuguese missionaries used to refer to the Lenten period and Christian holy days. Nowadays, chefs all over the world have embraced tempura and apply the dough and technique to various ingredients.

January 8
TOFFEE DAY

Made by caramelizing sugar or molasses and then adding butter and sometimes flour, toffee is a classic confection that continues to be loved today. Although its history is a bit unclear, it is believed it was invented in the nineteenth century, with the first mention appearing in 1825 in the *Oxford English Dictionary*. There are many different varieties, such as honeycomb toffee, almond toffee, and bonfire toffee.

English Toffee
with a Buttercrunch Twist

Makes about 2 pounds

INGREDIENTS

1 pound unsalted butter
1 cup water
2½ cups sugar
4 tablespoons corn syrup
2 cups milk chocolate chips
Chopped walnuts, optional

DIRECTIONS

1. Grease a cookie sheet and set aside.

2. Melt the butter in a large saucepan over medium-low heat. Attach a candy thermometer to the pan.

3. Once the butter is melted, add the water, sugar, and corn syrup.

4. Cook the mixture until it reaches 300°F on a candy thermometer, making sure to stir constantly so it does not burn.

5. Spread the mixture on the prepared cookie sheet. Sprinkle chocolate chips and walnuts, if using, evenly over the top.

6. Cool until hard. Use the back of a knife to break the toffee into pieces.

January 9
APRICOT DAY

While experts disagree over where apricots originated, with some suggesting Armenia and others China, what all can agree on is that this delicious fruit has been around for a long time. English settlers are responsible for introducing the apricot to the United States, and today California is the top-producing state, supplying almost 95 percent of our apricots.

FUN FOOD FACT
Apricot trees can produce fruit for up to twenty-five years.

{ *Women packing apricots in large, open sheds in Brentwood, California, 1938.*

January 10
BITTERSWEET CHOCOLATE DAY

{ *A man making cocoa bread, 1924.*

Bittersweet chocolate contains chocolate liquor (or pure cocoa from processed cocoa beans), sugar, cocoa butter, and vanilla flavoring. It has less sugar but more chocolate liquor than semisweet chocolate, but the terms "bittersweet" and "semisweet" are often used interchangeably in baking. The chocolate's packaging often lists the ratio of cocoa to sugar, with higher amounts of cocoa giving a more bitter taste.

January 11
HOT TODDY DAY

A perfect hot elixir for those cold and blustery days, hot toddies have been around for quite a long time, and were considered a home remedy for winter colds and the flu. The classic hot toddy includes one shot of whiskey, one teaspoon of honey, a dash of fresh lemon, and boiling water. Although some claim Scottish doctors invented the first hot toddy, food historians think that sugar and spices were used to disguise the rough flavor of raw scotch. There are thousands of variations on the hot toddy, with some using apple cider, chamomile, orange, and brandy or rum.

FUN FOOD FACT

During the "Golden Age of Piracy," bumbo—*a drink mixing water, rum, sugar, and nutmeg*—was a popular libation among the Caribbean buccaneers.

January 12
CURRIED CHICKEN DAY

Depending on the cuisine, the word "curry" can mean different things to different people. In England, "cury" was historically used to describe anything that was cooked and hot, the word being derived from the French *cuire*, meaning "to cook." In Southeast Asia, some believe that the word curry comes from the Tamil word *kari*, meaning "spiced sauce," referring to a thin sauce for dressing meats and vegetables. After chiles were introduced to India from Mexico and South America and added to curries, they became more nuanced and—sometimes—hotter. Today, we celebrate curried chicken, but let's also give special mention to all curries!

{ *Superior chickens being bred by government experts in Beltsville, Maryland, 1938.*

January 13
PEACH MELBA DAY

Australian native Dame Nellie Melba, born Helen Porter Mitchell, was a talented and internationally beloved opera singer who entertained audiences in the late nineteenth and early twentieth centuries in London and New York. Famous French chef Auguste Escoffier, who was the head chef at the luxurious Savoy Hotel in London, created four dishes in her honor: peach Melba, today's celebration, which is vanilla ice cream and peaches covered in raspberry sauce; Melba toast, which is crisp, dry toast; Melba sauce, a purée of raspberries and currants; and Melba garniture, which is a tomato stuffed with chicken, mushrooms, and truffles and topped with a velouté sauce.

{ *Dame Nellie Melba, ca. early nineteenth century.*

January 14
HOT PASTRAMI SANDWICH DAY

Developed as a means to preserve beef, pastrami (and, similarly, corned beef) is made by first soaking meat in a brine, after which it is dried, smoked with spices, and then steamed. The process results in extremely juicy cuts that go well with rye bread and spicy mustard. The word "pastrami" is derived from the Romanian word *pastramă*. Romanian-Jewish immigrants are credited with introducing this delectable method of preparing beef to the United Sates in the middle of the nineteenth century, and the legendary sandwich continues to popular in Jewish delis, with Katz's Deli in New York City being one of the top contenders for the best pastrami sandwich.

January 15
FRESH-SQUEEZED JUICE DAY

Whether orange, grapefruit, tomato, or pineapple, freshly squeezed juice is not only a refreshing way to start the morning, but also a healthy source of vitamins. Over the past twenty years, juice shops, home juicers, and smoothies have soared in popularity, making it easier for us to incorporate nature's liquid elixirs as part of our daily regimen!

{ *Congressional leaders receiving oranges from Old Gold and Sunkist in Washington, D.C., 1938.*

January 16
FIG NEWTON DAY

Up until 1891, when the first machine to pipe fig paste into dough was invented, fig newton "cakes" were made by hand. Massachusetts-based Kennedy Biscuit Company, which later became part of Nabisco, first manufactured Fig Newtons. Contrary to popular belief, Fig Newtons are named after the town of Newton, Massachussetts, not Sir Isaac Newton.

January 17
HOT BUTTERED RUM DAY

A cousin of the hot toddy, hot buttered rum dates to Colonial times and is typically made with butter, brown sugar, powdered sugar, spices, and, of course, rum. A Caribbean and Latin American import, rum became an extremely popular and cheap spirit of choice for the early colonists. The secret to a perfect hot buttered rum is to make a batter with the butter, sugars, and spices. Then, once the hot water is added, the butter does not rise to the top as film.

FUN FOOD FACT

While hot buttered rum was a pleasant and cozy way to warm up during the cold winter months in colonial America, these days its high calorie content make it much less popular.

January 18
GOURMET COFFEE DAY

There are two main coffee bean species: robusta, from the *Coffea canephora* plant (but commonly referred to *Coffea robusta*), and arabica, from the *Coffea arabica* plant. Robusta is sturdy, easy to care for, and gives a high yield, making it an affordable bean and a common ingredient in instant coffees and coffee blends. Arabica, on the other hand, is considered superior, as it is harder to grow, more sensitive, and lower yielding than robusta. Arabica beans have a softer and sweeter taste, while robusta has stronger and harsher notes. Regardless of your coffee preference, enjoy a cup of gourmet joe today!

FUN FOOD FACT

Robusta beans contain twice as much caffeine as arabica, which is the reason robusta beans are more bitter.

January 19
POPCORN DAY

{ *A family making popcorn in their living room fireplace, ca. 1970s.*

FUN FOOD FACT
There's ample archeological evidence that Mesoamerican societies used popcorn for eating as well as for ceremonial and decorative purposes.

Who doesn't love watching a great movie with a big bowl of buttered popcorn? Popcorn comes from a specific species of corn that contains small kernels with a hard shell. Once the kernel is heated, the moisture inside "pops" the kernel into a fluffy morsel. By the 1820s, popcorn became popular on the East Coast and was called Pearl and Nonpareil. In the 1890s, Charles Cretors from Chicago, Illinois, invented the popcorn maker by applying his nut-roasting technique to popcorn kernels. Although popcorn is synonymous with the silver screen, it wasn't until the 1930s that movie theaters began to offer their patrons this freshly popped snack indoors; prior to this time, vendors sold moviegoers popcorn from carts.

January 20
BUTTERCRUNCH DAY

Buttercrunch or toffee? Both names can refer to English toffee, adding yet a third term to a sweet and crunchy snack that continues to be popular today. Strictly speaking, however, English toffee is made with butter and sugar, but if plain English toffee is then coated with nuts or chocolate, it becomes buttercrunch. Almond Roca is the most popular type of buttercrunch in the United States. Produced since 1923 by Brown & Haley Company in Tacoma, Washington, Almond Roca is an almond buttercrunch topped with chocolate. Don't worry; if you eat English toffee today instead of buttercrunch, no one will know.

FUN FOOD FACT
According to company tradition, each Almond Roca batch contains a small amount of the original 1923 batch.

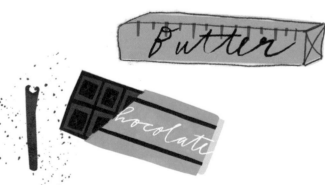

January 21
NEW ENGLAND CLAM CHOWDER DAY

Made with a base of either cream or whole milk, New England clam chowder is the perfect meal for blustery cold days. With some of the first references dating from the 1700s by French and Nova Scotian settlers, clam chowder has been served at Boston's Ye Olde Union Oyster House (the oldest continuously operating restaurant in the Unites States) since 1836. Manhattan clam chowder—its younger cousin, arriving on the chowder scene in the 1930s—uses a tomato base and is a popular variation. Although both versions are made using clams and broth, a true New England style contains only potatoes as vegetables.

FUN FOOD FACT

A number of critics have lambasted the Manhattan version over the years, with one legislator from Maine even attempting to outlaw tomato-based chowder in 1939.

January 22
SOUTHERN FOOD DAY

With roots in the European, Native American, and African-American traditions, Southern cooking is a truly unique American cuisine. Whether fried green tomatoes, okra, buttermilk biscuits, fried chicken, collard greens, or fried catfish, the list of Southern specialties is endless, and are all about home cooking and Southern pride!

{ *A man eating a homemade fried chicken dinner, ca. 1950s.*

FUN FOOD FACT
A true Southern staple, hushpuppies are fried balls of cornmeal that have an interesting story behind their name. Some sources believe that Confederate troops served the fried side dish to "hush" the dogs from approaching Union solders, while other sources claim the name originated from runaway slaves, who used hushpuppies to stop dogs from barking.

January 23
PIE
DAY

Americans are in love with pies. From Key lime to the classic apple, there are thousands of different types of savory and sweet dough creations. Pies have been around for thousands of years. The ancient Greeks are credited with developing the first pastry shells, and the ancient Romans made pies with all kinds of meat and seafood. In medieval England, *pyes*, as they were called, were usually filled with meat. In North America, pies were adapted to the native foods early settlers discovered in the New World, as well as various culinary traditions that immigrants incorporated in their newly adopted country. Whichever pie you choose today, enjoy it—preferably with a nice glass of cold milk!

FUN FOOD FACT

Even though apple pie was eaten in Europe long before America was colonized, the phrase "as American as apple pie" is still used everywhere—partly in reverence of the legendary American pioneer and conservationist Johnny Appleseed.

January 24
LOBSTER THERMIDOR DAY

Due to both its expensive main ingredient and its lengthy, complex preparation, lobster Thermidor is one of those rare old-school dishes that is a pure treat when found. This fancy dish, which includes a sauce of egg yolks and brandy, was first created in 1896 at Maison Marie, a well-known restaurant in Paris. The chef named the dish after the play *Thermidor* by Victorien Sardou. However, some accounts say that the famous chef Auguste Escoffier invented the dish in the 1880. Regardless of which tale is true, by 1907, the dish had reached the United States and was soon featured on the menus of top restaurants such as the Waldorf and Delmonico's in New York City.

January 25
IRISH COFFEE DAY

Made with coffee, Irish whiskey, and sugar, Irish coffee has a relatively recent history. In 1942, Joe Sheridan served American tourists hot coffee with Irish whiskey topped with cream at Foynes Airbase near Limerick, Ireland. He dubbed it "Irish coffee." Travel writer Stanton Delaplane brought the new coffee recipe back with him to San Francisco at the Buena Vista Hotel, where he and a bartender recreated the drink. It quickly became a popular item on their drink menu.

January 26
PEANUT BRITTLE DAY

Crunchy, sweet, and salty, peanut brittle has the perfect trifecta of flavor and texture all in one, but there are some conflicting histories behind its origin. Some say that in 1890, while making a batch of taffy, a Southern woman added baking soda instead of the usual cream of tartar. Instead of throwing out her failed taffy, she added peanuts and a new snack was created. Other accounts claim that peanut brittle was a Celtic-inspired dessert, which Irish immigrants brought with them to the United States.

FUN FOOD FACT

In Southern folklore, Paul Bunyan's cousin Tony Beaver saved an entire town from flooding by pouring peanuts and molasses into the river!

January 27
CHOCOLATE CAKE DAY

Whether flourless, German, Black Forest, or red velvet, chocolate cake is a perennial favorite. In 1828, Dutch chemist Conrad van Houten invented a process to extract fat from cocoa liquor to separate cocoa butter and cocoa powder from the cocoa bean, giving the world a cheaper version of chocolate. This "Dutch chocolate" ushered in new waves of chocolate use for all classes, since prior to this time, chocolate was only accessible to the rich. By the late 1880s, Americans began to add cocoa powder to cake batters, and the first chocolate cake recipes began to appear. The Duff Company from Pittsburgh, Pennsylvania, brought the first boxed cake mixes to the market in the early 1930s; however, cake mixes didn't take off until after World War II, when mixes requiring fresh eggs became popular.

FUN FOOD FACT

In 1948, Pillsbury introduced the first boxed chocolate cake mix.

Homemade Chocolate Cake

Makes 16 servings

INGREDIENTS

2 teaspoons white vinegar

2 cups whole milk

⅔ cup olive oil

1½ cups sugar

4 teaspoons honey

2 cups all-purpose flour

⅔ cup cocoa powder, sifted

2½ teaspoons baking soda

1 tablespoon espresso powder

Pinch salt

1 (16-ounce) container chocolate frosting

DIRECTIONS

1. Preheat oven to 350°F. Grease two 8-inch round cake pans.

2. In a small bowl, stir together the vinegar and milk together. Set aside to curdle.

3. In a large mixing bowl, whisk together the oil, sugar, and honey.

4. In a separate bowl, whisk together the flour, cocoa powder, baking soda, espresso powder, and salt until evenly mixed.

5. Add the wet ingredients into the dry ingredients, stirring until incorporated.

6. Divide batter evenly between prepared pans, transfer pans to the preheated oven, and bake for 20 minutes or until a toothpick inserted into the center of the cakes comes out clean.

7. Cool cakes for 15 minutes in the pans, and then remove cakes from the pans and transfer to a wire rack to cool completely.

8. Microwave frosting for 30 seconds, stirring to soften.

9. To assemble, place one of the cooled rounds on a serving plate and top with one-third of the frosting. Top with the second layer and add the remaining frosting to cover the outside and top of the cake.

January 28
BLUEBERRY PANCAKE DAY

{ *A woman making pancakes.*

Humans have been making pancakes—albeit rudimentary ones—since the Stone Age. The ancient Greeks and Romans used honey to sweeten their pancakes, while the medieval English preferred rosewater and sherry. The early American colonists called the first pancakes in the New World cakes, johnnycakes, and flapjacks, and they were usually made from buckwheat or cornmeal. Of course, any fruit is a perfect complement to pancakes, but blueberries add that sweet yet tart combination to one of America's favorite breakfasts . . . or dinners.

FUN FOOD FACT
The Algonquin Native Americans used maple syrup as a sweet drink.

Blueberry Pancake Madeleines

Makes 12 madeleines

INGREDIENTS

1 cup all-purpose flour
1 teaspoon baking powder
2 teaspoons granulated sugar
1 large egg, beaten
½ teaspoon maple syrup
½ cup whole milk
2 tablespoons unsalted butter, melted
½ cup blueberries
Powdered sugar, for sprinkling

DIRECTIONS

1. Preheat the oven to 375°F. Grease a madeleine pan.

2. In a large bowl, whisk together the flour, baking powder, and granulated sugar.

3. In a medium mixing bowl, whisk together the egg, maple syrup, milk, and butter.

4. Add the wet ingredients to the dry ingredients and mix until just combined.

5. Fill each madeleine cup half full and press 2 blueberries into each.

6. Transfer the pan to the preheated oven and bake for 14 to 17 minutes or until cakes are golden and the tops spring back when gently pressed with your fingertip.

7. Once cooled, turn the cakes out from the pan and sprinkle with the powdered sugar.

January 29
CORN CHIP DAY

Corn chips were first sold as *fritas*, a Mexican street food made by frying corn dough. In 1932, Charles Elmer Doolin from San Antonio, Texas, purchased the fritas recipe and equipment from Gustavo Olguin, a Mexican cook, and he transformed the idea into the Fritos empire that we know today. In 1945, the Doolin Frito Company partnered with Lay's, and the marriage was a successful one for both; by 1961 the two companies merged to form Frito-Lay. There are hundreds recipes that use corn chips, but one of the most popular is Frito pie, which uses a layer of Fritos chips covered with chili, cheese, and onions. The origins of this salty creation are contested, with Daisy Doolin, Charles's mother, getting official credit from Frito-Lay, while Teresa Hernández, a cook at Woolworth's in Santa Fe, New Mexico, also claimed to be the originator.

January 30
CROISSANT DAY

Brace yourself, folks: croissants are not originally from France! Most food historians concede that the croissant began in Austria as the *kipfel*, a crescent-shaped pastry made from butter (or lard), sugar, and almonds. (Some say the shape was a reminder of the Austrian victory over the Ottomans during the siege of Vienna, with the crescent representing the Ottoman flag, but older kipfel historical references debunk this theory.) References to the kipfel in France begin in 1838, when Austrian August Zang opened a bakery in Paris's Right Bank. His kipfel and other Austrian treats became a sensation, due to his ingenious advertising. Soon, there were many imitators, and the puffed pastry, which is a French invention, became the main ingredient. By 1850, the croissant, France's celebrated breakfast item, was born.

January 31
HOT CHOCOLATE DAY

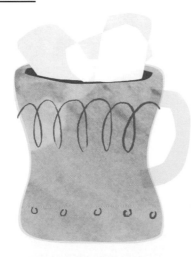

The first hot chocolate drink was consumed by the Olmecs, who lived in southern Mexico almost four thousand years ago. By grinding the cacao plant's nibs (the fermented, dried, and roasted cacao beans) into a paste and then adding hot water, the Olmecs drank what they called *xocolātl*, from which the word chocolate is derived. The Aztecs, who learned the recipe from their Olmec ancestors, considered hot chocolate to have both mystic and medicinal powers, and it was consumed only at sacred ceremonies. When the Spanish explorers arrived and conquered the Aztecs, they transported the chocolate drink (and the cacao plant) back to Spain, where it spread throughout Europe—and eventually started the world's love of chocolate.

FUN FOOD FACT
During the Revolutionary War, medics prescribed hot chocolate to wounded and dying soldiers, believing that chocolate had medicinal properties.

February

Food Celebrations This Month

National Canned Food Month

National Chocolate Lovers Month

National Cherry Month

National Grapefruit Month

National Snack Food Month

National Potato Lovers Month

National Hot Breakfast Month

National African Heritage and Health Week (First Week of February)

National Margarita Weekend (Third Weekend of February)

National Pork Rind Day aka National Pork Rind Appreciation Day ("Superbowl Sunday")

February 1
CAKE POP DAY

Want a bite or two of cake but not a whole slice? Cake pops fit the bill. Essentially cakes on a stick, these pops get their name from their resemblance to lollipops and are the perfect (almost guilt-free) snack! The secret to perfect cake pops is that they are usually made of cake crumbs mixed with icing, cream cheese, or chocolate and then formed into balls. Finally, they are either coated in rich icing, dipped in chocolate, or decorated with fun themes—no wonder they are so popular.

February 2
TATER TOT DAY

All hail the tot . . . the tater tot, that is. Who can say no to deep-fried cylinder-shaped potato bites? The ultimate processed food, tater tots were invented in 1953 by food engineers at Ore-Ida as a way of saving wasted potato bits. Americans now eat over seventy million pounds of tater tots every year. Other names for the tot include Tastie Taters, Spud Puppies, Oven Crunchies, and even Tater Toddlers.

February 3
CARROT CAKE DAY

{ *Workers from the Italian section of Philadelphia, Pennsylvania, arriving to work to pick carrots for the day in Camden County, New Jersey, 1938.*

When people think of having their vegetables, many would rather find them in a slice of cake with cream cheese frosting. Carrot cakes gained popularity in the United States during World War II when food rationing made it necessary to find new ways to sweeten cakes and breads; however, using vegetables as a sweetener dates back to Europe during the Middle Ages, when sugar was an expensive luxury item. English recipes for carrot "puddings" can be found as far back as the sixteenth century. Regardless of its origins, carrot cake continues to be one of the most popular cakes in the United States today.

FUN FOOD FACT
There are two main varieties of carrot: eastern and western. The much older eastern carrot was originally cultivated in Persia and is typically yellow or purple in color. The western orange carrot emerged much more recently in the Netherlands.

February 4
STUFFED MUSHROOM DAY

With an earthy taste and unique texture, mushrooms are a favorite ingredient for many cooks. Whether served as an appetizer or a main dish, they are guaranteed to always be a hit!

FUN FOOD FACT
Mushroom DNA is more similar to humans than it is to plants.

February 5
NUTELLA DAY

Due to post–World War II food rationing in Italy, cocoa was scarce, so chocolatiers used hazelnuts to stretch the chocolate flavor as much as possible. In 1946, Italian baker Pietro Ferrero created a chocolate bar using hazelnuts and a very little bit of cocoa, calling the resulting mixture "Pasta Gianduja," after a famous carnival character from the Piedmont region. It was an instant hit! Soon, a creamy spread was developed, and Nutella as we know it was born. Sales were so strong that in 1964 a factory was built and the first jars of Nutella were shipped. On its fortieth anniversary, World Nutella Day was declared. No recipe is needed for this delicious snack. Smear some Nutella on your favorite bread and enjoy!

February 6
CHOPSTICKS DAY

{ *A couple sharing noodles with chopsticks, ca. 1920s.*

Okay, yes, chopsticks may not be a "food" per se, but over a quarter of the world's population uses them daily. They first started appearing in China six thousand years ago and then spread throughout Asia. The English word *chopstick* received its name from the Chinese-American slang word chop-chop, meaning "quickly." In Japan, resting one's chopsticks over a bowl or plate is considered a major faux pas. In Korea, metal chopsticks are more common, and in Japan, wooden ones are preferred.

February 7
FETTUCCINE ALFREDO DAY

Pasta, butter, and cheese have been staples of Italian cuisine for centuries. The story behind this famous dish is that in 1914, Alfredo di Lelio, a Roman restaurant owner, served his pregnant wife fettucine with just butter and Parmesan cheese to soothe her nausea. It became an instant hit, and his restaurant became a top tourist attraction in Rome. However, most Italians know this dish simply as *fettucine al burro* (fettuccine with butter) or *fettucine al bianco* (fettucine with no sauce) and have been eating it for hundreds of years. Regardless of when it was "invented," today we know it simply as Fettuccine Alfredo, and it continues to be one of the most popular pasta dishes in the United States. What about Alfredo, you ask? Many still refer to him as "the emperor of fettuccine."

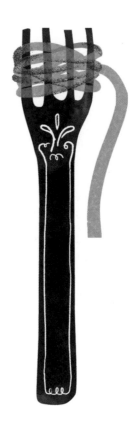

Classic Alfredo Sauce

Makes 6 servings

INGREDIENTS

½ cup (1 stick) unsalted butter
2 cups heavy cream
2 cloves garlic, crushed
3½ cups grated Parmesan cheese
½ teaspoon kosher salt
½ teaspoon ground black pepper
¼ cup chopped flat-leaf parsley

DIRECTIONS

1. Melt the butter in a large saucepan over medium-low heat. Stir in the heavy cream and slowly bring the mixture to a simmer, stirring constantly. Stir in the garlic.

2. Add the Parmesan and stir until the cheese is melted (small lumps are fine here).

3. Season with salt and pepper and stir in the parsley. Serve with your pasta of choice—fettuccine, today.

February 8
MOLASSES BAR DAY

Unfortunately, nowadays molasses has an unfair old-school reputation, but for hundreds of years it was extremely popular and used as a common sweetener in a variety of recipes. Molasses is made by extracting the juice of stalks of sugarcane or sorghum (labeled sorghum syrup or sorghum molasses), and then boiling it down into a syrup.

{ *Sugarcane juice being boiled into sorghum molasses in Racine, West Virginia, 1938.*

February 9
PIZZA DAY

Can you imagine pizza without tomato sauce? Well, the Italians ate theirs for centuries without it. It wasn't until the late 1400s, when Italian explorer Christopher Columbus brought tomato seeds back from his travels to the New World, that tomatoes were incorporated into European cooking. The word *pizza* likely got its name from the Latin word *pitta*, meaning "flat bread."

FUN FOOD FACT
The Celentano brothers invented frozen pizza in 1957.

February 10
"HAVE A BROWNIE" DAY

Like many classic American recipes, the exact source of the first brownie recipe is unknown, and there are many legends about its origins. Some sources cite a Mrs. Bertha Potter Palmer, a wealthy socialite, who asked her chef at the Palmer House Hotel to make "a dessert that could be tucked into a box lunch for ladies to eat while attending the Columbian Exposition [of 1897]." Others claim it was the 1897 edition of the Sears, Roebuck catalog that first mentioned a "brownie." What we do know is that by 1911, various recipes for these sweet treats were appearing in the extremely popular *Fannie Farmer Cookbook*. To whomever the lost creator is, we collectively thank you!

February 11
PEPPERMINT PATTY DAY

First created in 1940 by Henry Kessler in York, Pennsylvania, the iconic York Peppermint Patty was available only in the northeastern states until 1975, when it was bought by the Peter Paul Company, which then launched it nationally with the slogan "Get the Sensation." York was acquired by Hershey in 1988.

FUN FOOD FACT
All York Peppermint Patties had to pass the "snap test." If they did not break exactly in the middle when snapped open, they were rejected and sold separately at the manufacturing plant to local residents.

February 12
BISCOTTI DAY

Would you like a Roman army ration with your coffee? Stemming from the Latin words *bis* and *coctum*, this hard cookie's name means "twice baked," which harkens back to how they were originally made: to keep from spoiling while ancient Roman soldiers were traveling or en route to battle. Don't worry: dipping biscotti in a warm drink will resurrect them back into warm, gooey cookies.

FUN FOOD FACT

Biscotti *is the Italian plural form for "cookies";* biscotto *is the singular term for "cookie."*

February 13
"ITALIAN FOOD" DAY

Someone says, "Let's celebrate Italian food," and we immediately think, where to begin? There is no doubt that Italy has influenced our palate and our menus. Pizzas, as we know them, were perfected in the Naples area in the eighteenth century. Lasagna, one of the oldest Italian recipes, was traditionally made with layers of pasta sheets, meat, sauce, and cheese. Italians did not invent ice cream, but they have perfected it with their many flavors of gelato. There are so many more foods to list, from the numerous pasta dishes to focaccia flatbreads to the dessert tiramisu. Let's also not forget that Italy is the country that embraced coffee and perfected it with so many variations. So let's all shout a huge "Bravo!" to everything Italian!

February 14
CREAM-FILLED CHOCOLATES DAY

For centuries, people have expressed their love by sharing chocolates . . . and that's why Valentine's Day is also Cream-Filled Chocolates Day. Since the late 1800s, boxed cream-filled chocolates have been the perfect Valentine's Day present. Cadbury is considered to have been the first company to mass produce them in the United Kingdom. It wasn't until twenty years later that chocolate confectioners began to fabricate them in North America. Nonetheless, the question still remains: just how do they get the cream inside those hollow chocolate spheres?

February 15
CHEWING GUM DAY

{ *The packing department at the American Chicle Company plant, 1923.*

Many consider chewing gum to be as American as apple pie, but who knew that without Mexican president General Antonio López de Santa Ana, there might have never been chewing gum as we know it today? He presented chicle—a natural gum extracted from trees in Central and South America, which the Aztecs and Maya had been chewing for centuries to clean their teeth—to a New York investor named Thomas Adams, who incorporated the chewy new ingredient into his Adams New York Chewing Gum in 1871. Soon after, Black Jack, Chiclets, and Wrigley's Spearmint Gum became popular brands—and are still available today.

FUN FOOD FACT

The world's first coin-operated machine was made to sell chewing gum and was installed throughout New York in 1888.

February 16
ALMOND DAY

After being celebrated for millennia, of course almonds deserve their own day! The ancient Egyptians considered almonds a food from the gods, and the ancient Romans believed throwing almonds at wedding ceremonies would ensure fertility. Nowadays, almonds are found toasted, crushed, and even turned into milk.

February 17
CAFÉ AU LAIT DAY

This cozy, pleasant mixture of coffee and hot milk served in a porcelain cup is popular in cafés around the world, and though the term most often used in northern Europe and America is of French origin, many other countries have their own term for it. In fact, the Dutch term for this drink is *koffie verkeerd*—literally "incorrect coffee." In New Orleans, added chicory gives it a strong, bitter taste, which powdered sugar–dusted beignets served alongside it to help to offset the flavor.

FUN FOOD FACT

The French-speaking Swiss like to reverse the process of making café au lait, *adding espresso to hot milk to create* café renversé.

February 18
"DRINK WINE" DAY

Wine has been around since time immemorial, so why discontinue the tradition? Whether you prefer red, white, rosé, elderberry, honey, or rice wine, today we celebrate this fermented alcoholic beverage and the joy and revelry it has facilitated for thousands of years.

February 19
CHOCOLATE MINT DAY

Anyone who has tried Frango mint chocolate truffles, or the ever-popular Girl Scouts Thin Mints, can testify that mint and chocolate are the perfect couple. Mint takes its name from a nymph in Greek mythology, and since then, it has been a symbol of hospitality, with uses ranging from freshening banquet spaces, to deterring mice, to relieving chest pains. In tea houses and dinner halls of the early 1900s, mint sprigs and dark chocolates were served after desserts for patrons to "chew on for good breath and aid digestion."

FUN FOOD FACT

A variety of mint plant known as chocolate mint (mentha piperita) *evokes the flavor of Andes Chocolate Mints.*

February 20
MUFFIN DAY

Although English-style muffins, which use yeast or egg as a leavener, have been around since the eleventh century, American-style muffins are first mentioned at the end of the eighteenth century in *American Cookery* by Amelia Simmon, who included a few recipes for these quick breads, utilizing pearl ash as the leavening agent. Later, pearl ash would be replaced by baking soda (first produced in the United States in 1846 by Arm & Hammer) and baking powder (first produced in the United States by Rumford Baking Powder in 1857) as preferred leavening agents.

{ *A 1918 poster featuring canisters labeled as corn meal, grits, and hominy, 1918.*

FUN FOOD FACT
The Muffin Man was a real guy! He delivered muffins to homes along Drury Lane in England.

February 21
STICKY BUN DAY

Originating in Germany and introduced to American palates by the Pennsylvania Dutch, *schnecken* have been popular sweet roll treats since the Middle Ages. Before the leavened dough is pressed into the baking pan, sticky ingredients such as honey, maple syrup, sugar, nuts, and raisins are added to the bottom. This "sticky" part is always the best!

FUN FOOD FACT

The Venezuelan version of the sticky bun, called the golfeado, *ingeniously incorporates fresh cheese on top to make it a deliciously indulgent salty-sweet snack.*

Sticky Buns

Makes 12 to 16 servings

INGREDIENTS

2 small tubes refrigerated biscuit dough

3 tablespoons unsalted butter, melted, plus more for greasing pan

½ cup maple syrup

⅓ cup packed brown sugar

Pinch salt

½ teaspoon cinnamon

¼ cup chopped walnuts

DIRECTIONS

1. Preheat the oven to 375°F. Lightly brush a Bundt pan with melted butter.

2. In a small bowl, combine the remaining melted butter and maple syrup and set aside.

3. In another bowl, combine the brown sugar, salt, cinnamon, and walnuts.

4. Place half of the syrup mixture in the bottom of the pan. Sprinkle half of the brown sugar mixture on top. Lay the biscuits on the bottom of the pan, overlapping the edges to form a ring. Top with the remaining syrup and sugar mixtures.

5. Bake for 20 minutes, or until golden brown. Remove, then invert onto a serving platter. Let cool for 2 minutes, slice, and serve.

February 22
MARGARITA DAY

Like most drink recipes, the origins of the first margarita are numerous, murky, and span different decades. The one constant is the basic ingredients list: tequila, triple sec, and lime or lemon juice. Today, there are hundreds of variations. Authentic margaritas are made with Mexican limes (Key limes), which are smaller, thinner-skinned, and tarter than regular limes. Line up your playlist with some Jimmy Buffet and whip up this version for a quick Florida getaway!

FUN FOOD FACT
Some say the margarita is a version of a popular brandy-based Prohibition-era drink called the Daisy. In many Mexican border towns they swapped the brandy for tequila.

February 23
BANANA BREAD DAY

Banana bread, a quick bread, became popular in the 1930s, when not a scrap of food could be wasted. One of the first recipes was from Pillsbury. Americans began to eat bananas after the Civil War, as shipping methods became quicker.

FUN FOOD FACT
A cluster of bananas is known as a hand; each banana is a finger.

Margarita Fizz

Makes 8 servings

INGREDIENTS

1 (12-ounce) can frozen limeade, thawed to room temperature

1 cup water

10 ounces tequila

1 (12-ounce) can light beer of your choice

1 lime, cut into 8 wedges

DIRECTIONS

1. Pour all ingredients except lime wedges into a pitcher and stir. Serve on the rocks in chilled cocktail glasses, and garnish with lime wedges.

February 24
TORTILLA CHIP DAY

What would a good game of football or a casual family gathering be without tortilla chips? These corn-based snacks pair perfectly with nearly any kind of dip—although guacamole, pico de gallo, and chili con queso are the most common accompaniments. Add some cheese, sour cream, jalapenos, black beans, and other savory toppings and melt it all in the oven to create a tasty nachos dish. However you eat them, just remember that flavored varieties can pack a lot of extra salt.

FUN FOOD FACT

In 1966, Doritos became the first brand of tortilla chips with a nationwide launch in the United States. Their signature "nacho cheese" flavor debuted eight years later.

February 25
CLAM CHOWDER DAY

Whether New England-style white or Manhattan-style red, clam chowder has been around for a long time. Stemming from the French word *chaudière*, meaning "boiler" or "cauldron," our modern version has its roots in a poor man's fish stew, which coastal peoples have been cooking for thousands of years. One of the earliest mentions of an American chowder is from the *Boston Evening Post* in 1751.

February 26
PISTACHIO DAY

Pistachio nuts are a member of the cashew family and are closely related to mangos, sumac, and poison ivy. All pistachio shells are naturally beige in color, but many companies dye inferior nuts red or green. Iran produces more pistachios than any other country in the world with over two million tons per year.

February 27
CHILI DAY

There are countless chili recipes and hundreds of claims as to the most authentic chili recipe. Not surprisingly, mystery surrounds this famous Tex-Mex staple. One of the earliest written descriptions of *chili con carne* comes from a J. C. Clopper in 1828, who, although not mentioning the word "chili," wrote, "When [the poor families of San Antonio] have to lay for their meat in the market, a very little is made . . . it is generally cut into a kind of hash with nearly as many peppers as there are pieces of meat [which] is [then] all stewed together." By the 1920s, chili was a popular, well-known dish throughout the West. Legend has it that a seventeenth-century Spanish nun, Sister Mary of Agreda, experienced many out-of-body trances at her convent in Spain. After awaking from one of her episodes in which her spirit went to a distant place and met people who longed for Christianity and needed Spanish missionaries, she wrote down the recipe for chili con carne. Mysteriously, she was known to Southwestern Native Americans as La Dama de Azul, or the "Lady in Blue," yet she never traveled to the New World.

Cerveza Chili

Makes 6 to 8 servings

INGREDIENTS

3 pounds ground beef
1 tablespoon vegetable oil
2 red bell peppers, seeded and diced
1 yellow onion, diced (about 1½ cups)
2 cloves garlic, minced
1 jalapeño pepper, seeded and diced
2 poblano peppers, seeded and diced
2 (15.5-ounce) cans kidney beans,
   drained and rinsed
1 (16-ounce) can refried beans
2 (12-ounce) cans pale ale
1 (14.5-ounce) can diced tomatoes
5 tablespoons tomato paste
5 tablespoons chili powder
1 tablespoon cumin powder
Salt

DIRECTIONS

1. In a large pot or Dutch oven over medium heat, cook the ground beef until brown, 7 to 10 minutes. Drain and set meat aside.

2. To the same pot, add the oil, bell peppers, onions, garlic, jalapeño, and poblano peppers. Cook 5 to 7 minutes or until softened and lightly browned.

3. Add the drained meat back to the pot along with the kidney beans, refried beans, ale, tomatoes, tomato paste, chili powder, cumin powder, and salt to taste. Increase the heat to high and bring to a boil; then reduce the heat to low, cover, and simmer for an hour, stirring occasionally.

4. Serve alone or topped with cheddar cheese, sour cream, and diced onion.

February 28
CHOCOLATE SOUFFLÉ DAY

The king of fancy desserts, chocolate soufflé has caused many a chef to tremble when remembering their first attempt to making it. Soufflé comes from the French verb *souffler*, meaning "to breathe" or "to puff," and the secret to a perfect soufflé is perfectly beaten egg whites in a perfectly clean bowl. Frenchman Marie-Antoine Carême (1784–1833) is usually credited with today's modern version.

February 29
FROG LEGS DAY

Considered a delicacy in French and Chinese cuisine, frog legs are surprisingly popular worldwide. According to most accounts, the flavor resembles that of chicken, and the meat is packed with omega-3 fatty acids and vitamin A. Currently, Indonesia is the top exporter of frog legs, and recent estimates in frog leg production suggest that humans collectively consume about 3.2 billion per year.

FUN FOOD FACT
Because rigor mortis does not set in as quickly in frog muscles versus those of warm-blooded creatures, it's not uncommon for them to twitch while being cooked. (Yikes!)

Flourless Chocolate Soufflé

Makes 4 ramekins

INGREDIENTS

2 tablespoons butter, at room
  temperature
2 tablespoons caster (superfine)
  sugar
3 tablespoons heavy cream
2 ounces dark chocolate, chopped
1 egg yolk, at room temperature
¼ cup unsweetened cocoa powder
3 tablespoons cold water
4 egg whites, at room temperature
2 pinches salt
5 tablespoons granulated sugar

DIRECTIONS

1. Preheat the oven to 375°F. Prepare four 3½-inch ramekins by buttering the insides and sprinkling with caster sugar, knocking out the excess.

2. In a small, heavy-bottomed saucepan over medium heat, add the cream and stir until hot but not boiling. Remove from the heat, add the chocolate, and set aside for 1 minute.

3. While whisking constantly so as not to scramble the egg, slowly add in the egg yolk. Mix well until all of the chocolate has melted.

4. In a small, heavy-bottomed saucepan over medium heat, add the cocoa powder and cold water. Whisk thoroughly until well combined and close to boiling. Remove from the heat and allow to cool.

5. In a large bowl with a handmixer on medium speed, whip the egg whites and salt until light and foamy. Slowly add the sugar while continuing to mix until shiny and stiff peaks have formed.

6. With a spatula, scoop one-third of the egg whites into the chocolate mixture. Combine well. Then fold the chocolate mixture into the remaining whites. Spoon the batter into the prepared ramekins.

7. Bake for 15 minutes, or until the soufflé has risen about 1 inch above the rim. Serve immediately.

INDEX

6/18